Selected Poems

To
Caryl
with every good wish
Glyn

£6-
4r

GLYN JONES

Selected Poems
Fragments & Fictions

POETRY WALES PRESS
1988

POETRY WALES PRESS
GREEN HOLLOWS COTTAGE, CRAIG-YR-EOS ROAD,
OGMORE-BY-SEA, MID GLAMORGAN

British Library Cataloguing in Publication Data

Jones, Glyn, *1905–*
   Glyn Jones : selected poems, fragments
   and fictions.
   I. Title
   828'.91409

   ISBN 0-907476-85-6

Cover Painting: 'A Dyfed Farm' (1972) by John Elwyn.

Cover Design: Jeane Rees

*Published with the financial assistance of the
Welsh Arts Council*

Typeset in 10½ point Plantin by Megaron, Cardiff
Printed by Billings, Worcester

CONTENTS

I

II

The poems in Parts One, Two and Three of this book have been chosen from those that appeared in my previous volumes of poetry. Part Four has been written since the publication of my third volume, namely *Selected Poems*, in 1975. 'Prologue and Three Fragments' is part of a long unfinished poem called 'Seven Keys to Shaderdom'.

To that *Selected Poems* I added notes. In a widening awareness and an understanding of Welsh references these I have now omitted.

Many of these poems have appeared in magazines and anthologies in various parts of the English-speaking world.

Scene

This is the scene, let me unload my tongue,
Discharge perhaps some dirty water from my chest.

The north swells, bunioned with Pumlumon, whose
Side leaks water like some rusty old
Boiler's brickwork; his bleeding plait; cars at spring-tides
Line the river roads, switch headlights on, stroke
The stopped tide with car beams, finger the night bore.
That's Severn. Southward, beyond the bottled Channel,
England, Somerset, like foreign parts, and west,
John Masefield's notchy water, Cardigan Bay.

Circuited thus, my crumpled country lies.

The flat eyes of the Pembroke hawks discern
Zigzag coast-cliffs, three-ply islands, black rocks
Stuck bad-toothed and edgy from a blue-bag sea.
(One night not pinholed by a single star,
I lay half-frozen in the light-house field
And heard the fighting gulls, the prow-wash tide,
My body swept with big beams swung from Strumble Head);
Vine-veins of rivers flourish everywhere;
Some plains, paint-blistered into bolt-head hills;
The cloud-clawed mountains; prick-lark, a darkened star,
Drops, sees like a batter Beacon peaks,
Stiff, rough, stirred, gone solid-hard, rush up,
Fan Lleia, Fan Gihirych, Pen y Fan,
A wool road winding white along each pass.

You men who bus or walk for mart-day towns,
Bear baskets full containing fish or rabbits,
Are river-limers, clubbers of salmon,
I might have been, and liked it, born like you
Westward, or north, beyond the crooked coalfields.

But night on the Valleys and my first star stood
Voluble above those Beacon peaks,
Gesticulating like a tick-tack man.

Standing now where that birth-star was eloquent
I see my bitter county dawn between
My hands, I grieve above five valleys leaning
Suppliant against my unstruck rock;
I feel the mobbing flowers hug my feet,
The winds descend about my body, hoarse
As a garment, and my lonely burning flesh
Smokes up this sky-hook like a plunging fish.
Proudly I hail this pale past-sailing sun.

Town

And he watched from the cat-eyed bell-turret
The sea-smokes, and the flat town under them,
The sheety roofs, half blessed by this faint blue
Glove of mist, gently touching the Welsh flanks
Of distant hills with long divided fingers;
And the dome-leads, and the shining copper cocks
Circling the milky bulk of tomb-like towered clock.
Coal-smoke steamed across the lizard-crested
Ploughland of the near streets, and roofs
Patterned with a formal dew of slums.
St Peter's pinnacle was a sharpened pencil,
Towered Trinity a four-fanged tooth reversed,
St Paul's a ball and cross beneath a crowsfoot
Lightning conductor. Southwards, towards
The edgeless sea, six infant orange stacks
Issued in a row their sheepish smokes,
A soft snort of grey, like human breath.
Huge and brilliant on their tower,
Against the wipe of sun, gleamed the brass numbers
And the sworded face of that gigantic four-faced clock,
The burning morning oval of its rim.
Great cats dangle on the castle wicks,
The lemon lions of the marquis stir
Under the menace of black-breasted clouds.

Dock

Big sidings by the swing-bridge have black tons
Of trucked rock packed in twenty rows, sun-slavered
Coal converged upon the setting sun.
A black rat swims across the brass canal.

The sky tilts suddenly, its sleety herringbone
Of pouring rain spills thick across the dock,
Shags up the furry liner's side, its blurred
Black iron cliff immense above the dock-wall;
Pelts the sheety concrete, sprawls its gusty growths,
Its hiss of cold grey grass, across the tingling streets.

The gold coal-owner's daughter saves her hennaed
Hooks of hair, ducks pippin-breasted, slim grey-
Squirrelled, spindle-heeled, beneath some
Broker's porch; two big coal-trimmers, night-shift
Candle-pounds tucked dry, get after her.
One grins, "God lummy Charlie", and is silent.

Only one watcher herring-gull, turning
High up above the wetted town, sticks out,
His windy shoulder skilful in a storm
He saw ruled blue behind the Islands hours back.

Ship

Where were her grappled metals clenched in one,
The bolts stamped through her printed sides?
Where were the ways they struck her from, thrusting
Her screw-blades steep into the bulging waters?

Now she begins to stand in from the Roads, and
To set herself slowly towards the open caisson,
Putting her black prow in delicately between
The dreadful dockwalls, with the juddering siren
Fastened at her funnel-front spouting back
Thick steam. She moves slowly up the dock, half-
                frightened,
Into the tumult of her arrival — shouts,
Bell-clangs, bickering winches, the snarl of gulls
Rising off water-rings on the black dock water.
Tentatively she advances towards the harbour granites
Nervous steels along her doubtful sides, ponders,
Touches, draws back, resenting wheezing hawsers, and,
Finally, she settles quivering to the hushes of her berth.

She comes with eyes watching through tobacco smoke,
The harbour-master grumbling with plenty on his plate,
And the gulls lifting and falling on their way to sea,
Seeking a loophole in the wall of wind.

Shadow

Passing through tedium, through the city heat,
Bird-winged beyond those high panes, beating black
Across a vast, hot tilt of scaly church roof
Stretching opposite, swift isolation battering
Tight roof-slates plated thin in sun-slime, huge-
Winged upon the roof-pitch under pouring sun.
No shedding bird, blackback or Bishop's swan,
Only this swift shift, this fifteen foot black shadow,
Shed with more brilliancy than green moon's mail
Flung gold at full moon on the flinty water,
Sweeping its huge indifference past, its soundless
Spread of wings a black firm-crested breaker
Smoothing unbroken down the heaving roof, or thunder-
        rain,
Beyond all salutation of this shaken flesh.

Gull

Not tiring round the shores his rigid shadow, prompt
Beneath the landing webs that touch the sand;
Not kiting over-white against torn winds,
Milkily wheeling on brim-tilt wings, or heaping up   ·
Burnt breeze behind, with cutting air in ovals,
The long slant cornering, his steep-sloped, pointed wings
Speed-canted, speed-heeled over, leaned like skidding
          wheels.

But,
Behind the cape, day's great sun hits the sea;
Rain greys two blue bays; his flesh, his plumes
Flame-flushed, the burning gull flees, bearing fast
Fire, flashed out, launched across the flooded east;
Blush-feathered, frocked, above the grey-bled sea
He bears my beating heart with rosy webs,
The fire-bird, the flame-silked, through the grieving
          sea-rain, swift
On hot, flushed petal-flesh, his flashing wings.

Beach

Hears the heavy rising hay
   Dry-throat down his blade of land;
Hears the dim wind strum, strum,
   Behind the blushing bony wing,
Hears it from that sand-stuck wreck,
   That black smooth spoonful of sand.
Gazes up the bare beach, sees
   Pass again the slow bored gull,
The broken daisy-chain of rain.
   Grey razor-fine horizon cuts
Far beyond the deckless hull —
   Kissed (the sunset mouth-roof red,
The golden half-moon Gwil's hung glove),
   Kissed, Gwil, on the harelip twice,
Gwil, my love, my love.

Tree

The smudged west badged with Venus, then the moon,
(One bare, black beech, leaf-skeletoned against
Her unsunned, marigolden light), borne low
Over Merthyr like a cripple.
                                    Mayday;
The thrush, the throaty blackbird, ball-bounce and perch.
This grey beech breaks, the hindered sun, among
His great, unburied bones, climbs out beech green;
Low-louting boughs and sluggish, seaweed-swayed
Tall royals, all beechbud bespattered, are leaf-
Splashed as with startled mud-lace of burst bomb.

Ribboned in summer armour, his pierced shade
Drags peacock-marked with kingcups up the marsh,
Shedding his August leaf beneath my foot.
A blow-clock bent in autumn's wind-boil soon,
Bone-bare, a wooden skeleton; then bird-
Flocked over, thousand-hearted, starling fleshed,
Feeling roots' fistful of earth's breast hard ice.
Winter again upon his intricate white bones,
Waiting in Merthyr for the butchered sun,
His great heat torching upward melts his snow.

Choirs

Notched on the emigrating sun, the twin
Eggs of some tip-squatting collier's bum —
I saw the dole-queue climb that tip, the cops,
The blue-kissed working man, the shop-girl's mam.

And packed hot up their boxing stadium, I
Dreamed my train-scene while I ate my bread —
Sun-dodge, clucking siding-trucks, the huge green
Whale-browed Garth besunned his velvet head;

Remembering Cwmrhondda-Sospanfaching
Voices on the cheap side, singing beer,
Cuddling the Nile of sound between the steel
Lids of a needle's eye, my listening ear.

Their first song soft and sand-flow smooth — my blood
Broke into antish uproar, my tight throat locked,
Hearing that black-and-white-sexed, fanshaped choir-
Keyboard keening the sweet Handelian act.

> *Wie eine Heerde zog es hindurch.*
> *Herr, deine Hand schützte es,*
> *In deiner Güte gabst du ihm Heil.*

Remembering beside my Cardiff glass-
Edged lake — that high-blown, elm falsetto swills
Across the water, and the new moon's golden
Eyelash curves yellow on the singing hills;

Remembering the precious flesh, hymning
That honeyed hooey, those bloodshot fairy-tales,
I scare my blessings up with ruggered lungs like geese
Behind some honking king-goose over Wales.

Island

The tiny cream-bricked lighthouse on the hill
Glitters, seeing all and this. The island grass
Is silent and pale green, the high dry tide
Deep blue-wood water, smooth and shadowless,
Smooth to the white upright collar of the cliff.
One tealeaf swimmer swims that dusty sea.
Radiant and woollen gold, the sun sees too
The tilted gold-browed moon bent on the little park
Whose paths are heaped with snow, or burnt-wood black.
Over the velvet railings of the pond
A white-edged hunchback feeds a swan with cake.
The fancy bridge has bamboo legs, combs back
The river's long blue hair; and on its hump a boy,
Bald-headed, wearing lemon boots, leans back
Flying the fish-kite, while his Jessie sits
On gaudy grass to touch the raisin tree.
Pass, doves, and pass, you coal-flanked elephant,
Jessie's tall corn-coloured tree;
Make with your crimson satan-satin sash
Towards the glittering lighthouse, where the glass
Flashes its little lightnings in the sun.

Marwnad

The little oil lamp burns between us;
    It is made of blue glass;
Beside the bare table we sit waiting
    For the night to pass.

In the other room, through the open door,
    I can see him lying dead,
With his pit-clothes folded where they dropped them
    Beside the bed.

His mother watches the fleece of flame
    That grows over the embers,
Weeping softly for this, and those other griefs
    She half remembers.

My cheeks are dry for you, my man,
    But you know what's for me —
Even now I am wondering when my pains
    Will come upon me.

History

"Quick, come to the doorstep, Mother".
"What's to see there?" "Knee to knee
Cai the Prince and Car his brother
Riding down to Castelldu".

"I can't come now, our cake is baking".
"Oh, come quick, they've passed the door
With their ten gold banners shaking".
"Ach, I've seen it all before".

* * *

"Is this Castelldu, then, Mother?"
"This is Castelldu, my son".
"What's that — in that cage?" "His brother
Hangs there young Cai's skeleton".

"Let's go on, perhaps it's dropping
Finger-bones into the street".
"No, there's hardly time for shopping.
Turn here, son, to buy our meat".

Esyllt

As he climbs down our hill, my kestrel rises,
Steering in silence up from five empty fields,
A smooth sun brushed brown across his shoulders,
Floating in wide circles, his warm wings stiff.
Their shadows cut; in new soft orange hunting boots
My lover crashes through the snapping bracken.

The still, gorse-hissing hill burns, brags gold broom's
Outcropping quartz; each touched bush spills dew.
Strangely, last moment's parting was never sad,
But unreal, like my promised years; less felt
Than this intense and silver snail calligraphy
Scrawled here in the sun across these stones.

Why have I often wanted to cry out
More against his going when he has left my flesh
Only for the night? When he has gone out
Hot from my mother's kitchen, and my combs
Were on the table under the lamp, and the wind
Was banging the doors of the shed in the yard.

Song

I kept neat my virginity,
    No love gulled me to bed;
I whistled up the mountain stones,
    My unseen arms outspread —
Lustrous, the lord-star sprang to me,
    He was my son instead.

I felt my woody hair pour out
    Like water from my head
To see my nipples serpent-mouthed,
    My sucking star-child dead.

Gold

A midday half-moon slopes in heaven, tipped
And empty, with her golden liquor spilt.
She rolls transparent on the floor of heaven.
She has splashed her wine of gold upon the broom
And poured it over golden chain, adrip
With honey-drench, and emptied it between
My hands, where rests the gold-clot of my love's
Fair head, her chainmail cap of golden curls.

Sande

Sande's crucifix, that crisscross star.
The risking saint, naked and upright, scans
His crop of hills and prays against the dark.
The winds pluck off his ripened flesh like leaves,
And then his upright bone-shrub chants, the rigid
Thicket of his skeleton repeats
Its praises from a lip of bone, and through
The lantern holes of both his eyes, his ghost,
Erect and vivid, sees his morning star.
The melted lightnings yellow round his head;
The vigour of his dropped bones burns the rocks;
Scattered he prays and sees his pulsing star.

Stars

Stepping out at night expecting rain
Before the cold hostility of darkness,
I recoil confronted by the menace
Of the gathering stars. They stand out
In brilliance from their ambush, one by one —
Surrounded I surrender.

Night

This shadow flesh of risen man
Bears on my bones the blurt of pain,
Budges the rock and walks the quays —
The choking bandog snaps his chain.

Her upright body floats the tide,
Fish-teeth pluck her cheek-bones bare;
Naked Mary's candled wave
Blows in the harvest of her hair.

Mark the scandal on the hill
Before our feather-raided sea;
Sway like a bell-tongue, hanging man,
And fret your Judas-fruited tree.

The angelled air, the sea is edged
With fever where black Patmos lies;
Beneath his island aching oak
My thunder-hearted lover dies.

Like grief the rowdy swans return,
Rain has her earring on the thorn;
With broken hands I roll my rock
Back on the Pasc of this raw dawn.

Merthyr

Lord, when they kill me, let the job be thorough
And carried out behind that county borough
Known as Merthyr, in Glamorganshire.
It would be best if it could happen, Sir,
Upon some great green roof, some Beacon slope
Those monstrous clouds of childhood slid their soap
Snouts over, into the valley. The season,
Sir, for shooting, summer; and love the reason.
On that hill, varnished in the glazing tide
Of evening, stand me, with the petrified
Plantations, the long blue spoonful of the lake,
The gold stook-tufted acres without break
Below me, and the distant corduroy
Glass of the river — which, a mitching boy,
I fished — flowing as though to quench
The smouldering coalfield in its open trench
Of steamy valley, fifteen miles away.
Here, Sir, are more arrangements for that day: —
Lay me, lead-loaded, below the mourning satin
Of some burnt-out oak; the skylark's chirpy Latin
Be my *"Daeth yr awr"*; gather the black
Flocks for beaters — sweet grass their ham — upon the bac
Of lonely Fan Gihirych; let night's branchy tree
Glow with silver-coated planets over me.

And yet, some times, I can't help wondering;
Is this rather posh poetic death the thing,
After all, for somebody like me? I realize
I have a knack for telling bardic lies,
To say I see in some protean hill
A green roof, ship's prow, or an eagle's bill;
To claim the mountain stream for me's as clear
As flowing gin, and yet as brown as beer.
I fancy words, some critics praise me for

A talent copious in metaphor.
But this my gift for logopoeic dance
Brothers, I know, a certain arrogance
Of spirit, a love of grandeur, style and dash,
Even vain-glory, the gaudiest panache,
Which might impel to great rascality
A heedless heart. This glorying in all
Created things, the golden sun, the small
Rain riding in the wind, the silvery shiver
Of the dawn-touched birches, and the chromium river,
Innocent itself, has yet calamitous
And wilful pride for child and famulus.
And thus I see the point when puritan
Or mystic poet harried under ban
Sensual nature, earth, sea and firmament;
I apprehend some strain of what they meant,
And look at nature with a wary eye.
Sir, that death I sought was pure effrontery.

Lord, when they kill me, let the job be thorough
And carried out *inside* that county borough
Known as Merthyr, in Glamorganshire,
A town easy enough to cast a slur
Upon, I grant. Some cyclopean ball
Or barn-dance, some gigantic free-for-all,
You'd guess, had caused her ruins, and those slums —
Frightening enough, I've heard, to daunt the bums —
Seem battered wreckage in some ghastly myth,
Some nightmare of the busting aerolith.
In short, were she a horse, so her attackers
Claim, her kindest destination were the knackers.
Yet, though I've been in Dublin, Paris, Brussels,
London, of course, too, I find what rustles
Oftenest and scentiest through the torpid trees

Of my brain-pan, is some Merthyr-mothered breeze,
Not dreams of them — a zephyr at its best
Acting on arrogance like the alkahest.

An object has significance or meaning
Only to the extent that human feeling
And intellect bestow them. All that sensational news
The heart hears, before she starts to bruise
Herself against the universe's rocky rind,
Is what she treasures most — the sight of wind
Fretting a great beech like an anchored breaker;
The vale, pink-roofed at sunset, a heavenly acre
Of tufted and irradiated toothpaste; the moon
Glistening sticky as snail-slime in the afternoon;
Street-papers hurdling, like some frantic foal,
The crystal barriers of squalls; the liquid coal
Of rivers; the hooter's loud liturgic boom;
Pit-clothes and rosin fragrant in a warm room —
Such sensations deck a ruinous scene
(To strangers) with tinsel, scarlet, spangles, green,
Gold, ribbons, and the glare of pantomime's
Brilliancy in full floods, foots and limes.

But far more than the scene, the legendary
Walkers and actors of it, the memory
Of neighbours, worthies, friends and relatives,
Their free tripudiation, is what gives
That lump of coal that Shelley talks about
Oftenest a puff before it quite goes out.
My grandfather's fantastic friends, old Sion
O Ferthyr, occultist, meddler with the unknown —
(The spirits in malevolence one night
Nigh strangled him, but sobered Sion showed fight!)
My grandfather himself, musician, bard,

Pit-sinker, joker, whom the Paddies starred
As basser for their choir — so broken out!
My undersized great granny, that devout
Calvinist, with mind and tongue like knives;
The tall boys from Incline Top, and those boys' wives;
The tailor we believed a Mexican,
A rider of the prairies; Dr Pan
Jones (he it was who gave my father
The snowy barn-owl) Bishop — *soi-distant* rather;
Refined Miss Rees; Miss Thomas ditto; Evan
Davies, and the Williamses from Cefn.
Sir, where memories, dense as elephant
Grass, of these swarm round, in some common *pant*
Or hilltop lay me down; may the ghostly breeze
Of their presence be all my obsequies;
Not sheep and birds about me, but lively men,
And dead men's histories, O Lord. Amen.

Hills

Down under the gloom on the cold floor
Of the forking Valley, among the villages,
Each a little mound of glow-worm lights,
The men that passed me by lie buried
Under this load of darkness deepening.

I have stood aside when they flooded down
The slope from two pits, the sound of their boots
Like chattering of tipped hail over roofs;
I can remember like applause the sound
Of their speech and laughter, the smell of their pit-clothes.

On the hill-top, ambushed by rising stars,
Beneath a pine-tree giving up its scent
Into the night like some monstrous blossom,
A man stands suffering, with tears salt
And cold upon his mouth for very pity.

Again

Lamplight from our kitchen window-pane
Shines out on the leaves of the little apple-tree
Dripping in the rain.

Inside the warm room, those two women together
Cleaning the brass candlesticks in silence
Are my daughter and my mother.

She has become a woman to me, my daughter,
Her dress heavy with her breasts, her arms heavy;
She is desired now, she is a lover.

But what will have come to her, and been hers,
Her crooked hands idle on the table
And her feet slow on the stairs?

Her granny, tired out, her mouth dropped open,
Sits with her eyes shut, facing the lamplight.
She has seen so much happen.

Shall my daughter too run through the streets to the
                          pit-head,
And stand cold among the women crowding the gateway,
And see the young men brought up dead?

Morning

Now it begins, though God knows why.
—Beneath my blind a rich blue sky —
Shamed and sick, my soothed heart knows
The sweet, soft, explosions of the rose.

—Today floats molten, its gold froth chars
The oblong, set with three stone stars
And looped with a new moon's silver wire —
My null flesh torches forgotten fire.

—Three from the dawn, three blazing swans
Flash it off their migrant bronze —
I hold this moment — *the sun's afloat! —*
My murderous life, God, by the throat!

Cwmcelyn

His wings blissful in a silent drumming
    Of beautiful sunlight, the buzzard. Below him,
    The estuary; below him the hills,
Green fields with the hay gone; the cornfields,
Silent and sunburnt encampments
    Of wheat-stooks; below him the tranquil
    River, gently heaving the mirrors
Afloat on her surface; below him
These woods, where flashes the grey pigeon,
    White in the paint of her flying.
    Below him Cwmcelyn, the farm.

Now the griefs of that homestead are mine.
    Drunken, in anger, or passion,
    Dejected, trampling this warm web-work of shadow
Between village and farm, my blood,
Through long generations, bore their flesh.
    Let me not, in the repose of this sunlight,
    Tranquil on fields and on heaving estuary, see
Their symbol and image; or falsify
Toiling and poverty, rebellion
    And bitterness of theirs to a pastoral
    Heaven. Defilement was theirs, and folly,
Suffering, questioning, and death. And yet,
Between them and the eternal, a harmony.

Soon shall I leave these swarthy cornfields,
    The dawdling gull and the grave river, for
    The acrid city, where the body of the burnt
Saint smoked in its unavailing martyrdom;
Where now the sacrifice of love is not enjoined;
    For the talk, for the belittling fool,
    For the annihilation, for no God,
No king, no shrine, no sanctuary.

Whose is the name to which every knee
    In that city's empty-hearted wilderness
    Shall bow? Ghostly reapers of Cwmcelyn,
You arraign them, the demoniac folly,
The soul's dissonance, and the despair.

Watcher

At the end of the field here I have waited, and am waiting;
The eastern clouds behind the trees are soaked in
                blackness,
And stars come out and ripen in the clear stretches of sky.
How long shall I wait for your coming out of the waters?

The black sea beyond the field is smooth as a river,
And the red reflection of a buoy-light writhes there;
Far on the left, five fields away,
The lighted village stretches out like a glowing filament.

When shall I see you coming up golden before me,
Coming warm and full between sea and sky,
With the heavens, moon of the south, golden-green about
                you;
When shall I see you rising warm out of the waters?

Linnet

Green from the going sun the linnet fell, and swayed
To a silver flash new wire in my garden fence.
The sun burned green upon his round warm breast, the
        wire
Frayed a little fringe of feathers as he swung.
Clinging, he glanced bright-eyed about, and then flew off,
Spreading his wings, as though to make a trustful jump
Into awaiting arms, and the empty wire thrilled
Behind him with his little kick. I wish that he had come
And perched upon my finger, I wish I could have felt
The weight and tightening of his little gripping hands,
And the gentle rubbing of his breast against my finger.

(From 'Maelog the Eremite')

High Wind in the Village

The clouds go grey for snow or sleet,
The blown gulls beaten about our street,
Where the lad I'd love to wed
Paints his black boat black and red.
I hope my mop of hair will lie
Tidy till I've passed him by.

Returning

At the window is the shine of the large wet leaves.
I must go to father and son in their boat as it heaves
Gently in the rain. I must speak before it leaves.

The young man at the stern with yellow hair
Sits silent in the dusk with his head and hands bare.
Soon at the thin sea I shall be speaking to him there.

Their mast lamp is lit. I must speak before night comes on.
The last gull rises now from its ring upon
The heaving water, rises over the roof and is gone.

I must leave the dim window, I must call across the shore.
A shadow touches my feet over the darkening floor;
It is the son returning, he stands at my open door.

Easter

Morning in the honey-months, the star
Of annunciation still lit in the sky,
Upon me fell the heavy unpinned hair
Of apple, perfumed almond, pear,
With dawn-chorus, dewfall, and the incarnate
Promise of the primrose flesh in bloom.

Leaving the morning garden, I sought the room,
The bedside of a woman winsome to me
Once, though old, clean in her white cap, comely
In candle-light, or the green shine of stars.

In death's stink now, with tears I watch her, old
And hideous in her dying — bitterly
She moans, her face death-dark, her tangled hair
Tortured behind her little rolling head.
She wakes a moment, calming our kindling room,
Opens untroubled eyes, and lifting up
Bone arms like glistening sticks, prays for the droll
Child of her weeping sailor. Anguish returns;
Again she moans — it is the grave-bound flesh
That grieves — but soon now must remission come
Upon the agony of this endured embrace,
Soon must the flesh rot in its stony bed.

Now, with a burning in the east, the breeze
Curves across the young cheek of the day;
Soon shall the thrush be at his crowing point,
Frailer than filigree the stems begin to bud;
Soon over grooved fields shall grow the soft
Plush-pile of the grass-like wheat, the green
Velvety nap of springing corn burst forth —
Soon, soon, the doors of every grave shall open
And the light of dawn shall shine upon the dead.

Ladybird

A smoke-stack spreads its sullen foliage low
Over the laden town. Splashed black
Raindrops spot our painted sill;
Ladybird-skin, she says, but dumbed with wind,
Plastering across our gusty window-glass
The ample wet hair of the pouring rain.

This is an autumn. The spring's ill wind
Lynched beeches, bled my finger-nail
A loaded ladybird, that afternoon
I lay, lonely, in love, along the sea-dyke,
Beneath a beech, a branch lush in the wind,
And gazed beyond the varnished grasses, at
The glitter, at the sea, the flame-fine sails
Blown across the burnish, while our beech
Mewed above us, cat-voiced and inveterate,
And all your hair, frantic in golden curls
Fingering my face, towards the green
Mockery of your eyes beckoned me down.

And, over my eyes in perfume, my wound
Yelled — that summer silver-coated night
Of boughs, after the rains, after the stars
Crowded the sky, after the low moon
Was corn-gold and assured among
The birch-twigs and the sycamores.
Darkness was poured perfume, and under ban
Its voices. At my words to you, trees, earth,
And glitter clicked into rigid fixity,
And all the night yammered, and the blade
Of your rebuke was vast in my body
And I bled. She, the punctured ladybird,
Burst on my gunshot-thimbled agony,
Clad in the small confetti of her wounds.

Here, against the gusts, our fire glows.
The easy spittles of our little clock
Chew time up for us, sweet as a cud.

Ambush

Midnight, and the new moon sunk.
Into the wood the soldier peers.
In dread and dark the forest seems
An army resting on its spears.

Oh, hostile spears, spare this boy,
In anguish now, before the fight,
Butchering fears who find his heart
Their forest and their moonless night.

He hears the crash, and sees the glare
On rocking trees and quaking land.
One dewdrop, in a gentle curve,
Falls, a soft jewel, upon his hand.

A new throb thunders through his heart;
He lies in stupor at this sign;
In death and dark, the eternal pause
Is proffered now, like bread and wine.

And now, with ghostly eucharist,
He feels the heavenly hungers fed;
For him, on grave and heaving ground,
The auguries of love are spread.

The Seagull

(after Dafydd ap Gwilym)

Gracing the tide-warmth, this seagull,
The snow-semblanced, moon-matcher,
The sun-shard and sea-gauntlet
Floating, the immaculate loveliness.
The feathered one, fishfed, the swift-proud,
Is buoyant, breasting the combers.
Sea-lily, fly to this anchor to me,
Perch your webs on my hand.
You nun among ripples, habited
Brilliant as paper-work, come.
Girl-glorified you shall be, pandered to,
Gaining that castle mass, her fortalice.
Scout them out, seagull, those glowing battlements,
Reconnoitre her, the Eigr-complexioned.
Repeat my pleas, my citations, go
Girlward, gull, where I ache to be chosen.
She solus, pluck up courage, accost her,
Stress your finesse to the fastidious one;
Use honeyed diplomacy, hinting
I cannot remain extant without her.
I worship her, every particle worships!
Look, friends, not old Merddin, hot-hearted,
Not Taliesin the bright-browed, beheld
The superior of this one in loveliness.
Cypress-shapely, but derisive beneath
Her tangled crop of copper, gull,
O, when you eye all Christendom's
Loveliest cheek — this girl will bring
Annihilation upon me, should your answer
Sound, gull, no relenting note.

The Dream of Jake Hopkins

(A poem performed on radio)

PART ONE

JAKE

(*Slowly*)
Here I stand, a middle-aged master,
My hair like tow and my face like plaster,
Awaiting my class — and awaiting disaster.

This is my register, where crimson rain rages,
The ink-strokes a downpour no thinking assuages,
And daily I drown in the rain of these pages.

For forty names I must mark every morning,
The earlies in red and the late ones in mourning;
For those who've been absent, I must work up a warning.

The bell-tower booms for the school-day's beginning.
But I hear in its thunders an under-bell tolling
For the heart in me dead, and diurnally dying.

Here I sit staring, a has-been teacher,
Behind my moustache, like a straw-haired Nietzsche.
All is vanity, I say with the preacher.

(*Briskly*)
All stand, all still, all silent, all sit.
You mustn't smile, you mustn't sneeze, you mustn't
     scratch, you mustn't spit.
Keep clean, keep cool, keep sweet, keep still.
Don't be late, don't be lazy, don't be lousy, don't be ill.
Never mitch, never moan, never cry, never quit.

You'll be famous, you'll be wealthy, you'll be worthy,
            you'll be IT!
        ALL SIT!

(*Slowly*)
Here I scowl on a sad Monday morning,
Cross as cats'-cradles — but my Bashan-bull bawling
Is counterfeit only — the soul of me's yawning.

(*Brisker*)
But here comes my headmaster, the great I AM,
His leering visage brazen as Birmingham,
Like a fanged grin off the roof of Notre Dame.

HEADMASTER

(*Sotto voce*)
I am the sole headmaster of this school.
I know that Hopkins here thinks I'm a fool.
Fool or no fool — this much must be said —
Hopkins is still a teacher — while I'm a head.

(*Aloud*)
Good morning, Mr Hopkins. Good morning, all you boys.
Now get on nicely with your work, and get on without
            noise.
Revise your money tables, and length, and avoirdupois.

Now, Mr Hopkins, may I see your weekly record book?
Is that your yearly syllabus? I'd like to have a look.
When you mark your dinner register, I hope you check the
            cash,
Because though these boys can't do their sums — they'll

52

cheat you in a flash.
This lad I see is absent — you should have put a dash.
I expect you've marked your papers, and got your lists
                    prepared,
Of the terminal exams, to show how every boy has fared,
And drawn nice red-ink brackets on them where a place is
                    shared?
Now your file of record cards — I very much deplore
That my teachers look on filling them as something of a
                    bore.
I hope you'll do your forty, Mr H, by half past four.
Then from this left-hand column — could you calculate for
                    me
All those boys who'll be thirteen plus in nineteen sixty-
                    three?
And the boys who write left-handed, for filling form C3.
That only leaves the savings. Is there anything I've missed?
Oh yes, the number present — and the requisition list —
And a list of all addresses — and the ages in a list —
And a list of all boys absent — and a list of every list
That you've listed in your thirty years of list begetting list
List, list, list, list, list, list, list . . .

JAKE

A scowl and a bawl and the boys drop their larking
And attend to this rigmarole, register marking.
Twice a day they and I must endure this clerking.

A is for Andrews, who climbs a club table
And sings every night there in heavenly treble;
No wonder his peaked face is pale as a pebble.

B is for Billo, in cassock and puttees;
He terrifies all who might jeer at these tatties
By his lunatic laughs as he beats up his butties.

C is for Claud with the kick of a broncho;
D is a Dai-cap who always lies doggo;
And Eddie's a blusher who'll sing nothing solo
Though his notes are as sweet as the voice of bel canto.

Fred climbed the pylon that holds the high tension;
He saw the red notice but paid no attention.
Now Fred's a peg-leg, it's important to mention.

Gwyn's a bird-watcher, and Harry a smiler;
Id is my top boy, and Jim a half-miler;
Ken, in no underclothes, is tough as a tiler.

What I note in young Len is his love for a Woodbine,
And soaped hair combed up like the blades of a turbine.

Murphy's home is a ruin, with one double-bedder
For swarms of young Murphys, the younger the madder.
Now their stairs have collapsed they go up on a ladder.

N — Neville sells newspapers, knows all the angles.
Why is he wearing green gloves with bright spangles?

Oliver also — he leans out to starboard
Through hawking round newsprint for Gulp, Son and
                    Cardboard.

P — Peter, big bosomed — that swollen pullover
Holds comfort for conies — clean shavings and clover.

Quintin's our fatty, our fool and first-aider;
When he treated Len's cut he bound up the wrong finger.

Fifty lengths of the baths are no burden
To neatest and sweetest of swimmers, Riordan.
But he's clumsy in classrooms as gulls in a garden.

Stan has been fighting — his eye and its fellow,
Like the signs of the A.A., are black and chrome yellow,
Though his nose remains trim as the nose of Novello.

In his daydreams Tom hands around jewels and sables
To a lure of Lamours and a glamour of Grables;
But it's strong horses' work to teach Tom his times-tables.

Ungoed too is a dreamer — that flat medallion
Of face hides a victor astride a white stallion,
Or a prince who elopes with a girl and a galleon.

V is for Vernon and Verdun his brother,
Spoilt by a late start and too-loving mother.

And Wayne's granny Williams is just as adoring;
She keeps a sly brothel and lives on the whoring,
But instead of being spicy her talk is plain boring.

The keen and the cosy, the lout and the limber,
The blond and orbicular, the eager for slumber,
XYZ are others who make up the number.

Here hops my boss like a voluble vulture,
Trying to talk with the accents of culture
To a person with French hands, and eyes always darting,
And hair split in two in a beautiful parting.

HEADMASTER

(*Sotto voce*)
I am the sole headmaster of this school.
I hope that Hopkins here keeps calm and cool
When I introduce to him this lucky one —
An inspector young enough to be his son.

INSPECTOR

(*Aside*)
Scaffolding bristles about a block of new
Flats, or offices for Pearl or Pru;
I am the new inspector. Authority
Is the hedgehog scaffolding that bolsters *me*.

(*Aloud*)
Good-day, Mr Hopkins; so this is your class!
I hope that you don't try to teach them *en masse*,
But cater for each individual boy —
Not progress for Percy and stasis for Roy.

JAKE

Mr Inspector, attention to each
Is for those who have fourteen, not forty, to teach.
Yet forty are learning, the skim with the cream,
When they sing in a chorus, or play in a team.

INSPECTOR

Quite, quite, Mr Hopkins, but don't you agree
That much of our teaching would bore you and me?

JAKE

Boredom, Inspector, like measles, I hate.
But measles are destiny, boredom man's fate.
This room I conceive of as no Tir na n-Og
Where virtue comes easy to poltroon and rogue,
And where duffers — your pardon — the retarded child,
      can,
Playful and sweatless, become the wise man.
Ineluctable three for all those who draw breath
Are boredom, the tables to twelve-times — and death.

INSPECTOR

Come, come, Mr Hopkins, this must be a pose.
Only some tight-collared colonel, who shows
At club windows the whiskey-red shrubs of a nose
In a face more empurpled than John Ruskin's prose
Could adhere to views so outmoded as those.

JAKE

My views are outmoded? Now what can that mean?
I know that in my job, what shall be — has been.
As a child, sir, I stood in the fairground, enthralled,
As the calliope blorted, the hoop-la lads bawled
And the naphtha flares shone on the chic and the shawled.
I gazed at the roundabout — horses and bears,
Ostriches, zebras, in Noah's Ark pairs
Flashed rising and falling past the bright flares.
But always I fancied one cream broncho best.
My love was exclusive, I ignored all the rest
As he came where I waited on roundabout mud
With a shine for my eyes and a thump for my blood;

Snorting, his mane in the winds of the west,
His eyes lidless jewels, red gems on his breast,
My galloper came at my silent behest.
Now for thirty odd years, to this slum class-room station,
That merry-go-round that we call education
Has brought its new theories, a zoo-full of creatures,
To the eyes of experience, most with good features,
To the eyes of maturity — not one conclusive.
Learning from books came here, close correlation,
The project, the play-way, complete self-expression,
They came and they went like the gingerbread bears
And the camels and cocks in the roundabout flares;
Yet each to *some* theorist was final, exclusive,
Absorbing, enthralling, enchanting, fulfilling
As that cream-coated mustang on which went my shilling;
Even those crazy as creatures from 'Alice'.
Do you wonder, Inspector, — I speak without malice —
That I take all their theories now *cum grano salis*?

HEADMASTER

(*Aside*)
I am the sole headmaster of this school.
Hopkins does damage with this silly drool.
Also, never to quarrel is my rule.

(*Aloud*)
Mr Inspector, next door's a man called Clissett,
A modern, young and eager teacher. Is it
Your pleasure that we pay his room a visit?

PART TWO

JAKE

I, Jacob Hopkins, B.A., middle-aged, but still
In good health, that is, never physically ill,
Marvel at this thirty year regarded slumland scene
Outside my window. What can it mean? What can it mean?
Here, in the sunlit school, all is still, as though
Midnight had moved into it. The boys,
Heads bowed in quiet absorption, write
At forty desks. Through large open windows
Sunlight like an airy liquor fills the room
And lays along the knotted floorboards lit
Oblong mats of sunglow. A boy coughs.
Clink, goes a naily boot against an iron.

Passing the open window, an old crow comes
Hawking his man-size croak around the afternoon.
What can it mean?
                Outside, sunshine is sheeted
On the slaty tillage of the slum-street roofs.
A factory stack emits a curved black horn
Of crinkled smoke. Little shrubs of steam break out
Along the river wharves, and the river skin
Burns in the snow-light of its silver fire.
All that I see but feeds my ignorance.
I cannot penetrate this shell, my glance
Shatters on the tough plate armour of appearance.

VOICE OF BLESSED MEMORY

There is no need to penetrate for what you seek.
I, like Noah's pigeon, bear green leaves in my beak.

They deck the trees of childhood. Let me perch and speak.

JAKE

Green leaves must mean those childhood boughs are high
              and dry
Not drowned out by the endless bawling of the sky.
Shall I laugh at what you tell me — or maybe cry?

VOICE OF BLESSED MEMORY

Do you remember the grandmother of those days?
Do you remember, when the whole sky was ablaze,
And the crimson sun-ball, evulsed and fiery, stood
Dissolving on the hillcrest? A heavy figure, broad
And black, floated out of that bonfire, as it were
Upon a rolling raft of warm illumination.
Slowly, encumbered and laborious,
She shepherded her shadow down the slope,
Her cloakful of vast flesh, with the ponderous budge
Of each slow, clog-clad foot, swaying against
The great out-dazzling hump of hilltop radiance.
Returning from her prayer meeting, she, your Nain,
Wore her long black boat-cloak; on her head her black
Cloth hat darkened her swarthy features, alien,
Wrinkled like grain in wood, and the down-bent
Cartwheel brim brushed the broad spreads and
              superstructures
Of her shoulders. She reached her garden rowan tree
And eyed with mildness, love and benediction all
The wide sweep of the mining valley. Then, turning back,
Looked at the cut sun and the after-glow, her guttered face
Lit up like a rock of clear crystal, her body,
Black and opaque, glowed warm, while momentary

Light and starlight inhabited her glistening skirts.
With shouts and singing limbs you reached her side,
She was your radiant Nain, your glossy one, whose harsh
Fingers were gentle as a harp-hand on your curls.

JAKE

Yes, I remember innocency's ecstatic hill,
Where of good and loveliness I received my fill.
But who are you, squawking on my slum-school sill?

VOICE OF UNDESIRED MEMORY

I carry memories too, but not from golden wheat
The bread I bear. My beak brings crusts to eat.
I am of the ravens that brought the Tishbite meat.

JAKE

At Kerrith brook, even prey-bird gifts were sweet.

VOICE OF UNDESIRED MEMORY

Do you remember in her dim, sweet-smelling kitchen,
Your Nain, by the fire, with those mangled hands
Held heavily upon her aproned knees? Large, red
And rugged, old, their gnarled erubescence
Manifested long familiarity
With rough toil, and coarse clay seemed an element
Of their conformation: the backs were twisted
And incised, the bony knuckles large,
Inflexible, the powerful inflammatory fingers
Ringed, and grooved with lines, like roots
Thick from the soil. Did you ever think what tasks
Those haunting hands fulfilled in her childhood poverty?

VOICE OF MEMORY'S VARIANCE

Jake's granny said that Jake never should
Play with the pagans in the wood.
The wood was bright, the grass was green,
And in came a countess with a tambourine.
Jake took her to the shore to get a ship to France
But he lost her to a sailor in the farewell dance.
As he ran home to his granny, he though his heart would
      crack,
So he cried along the roadways, "Nain, oh take me, take me
      back,
Take me back, oh take me back . . ."

VOICE OF BLESSED MEMORY

Do you remember an ecstasy of health and learning?
Do you remember in cheap college lodgings
The arguments on art with Tom and Barty,
The arguments on faith with Dave and Nico,
The arguments on politics with Jyder
Davies, Billy Handel, Bobby, Chewzie Hughes,
The arguments on sex with everyone?
Do you remember sitting in the long-room smoke
Of a grim suburban pub, after the match,
Your team, in their own fetor, steaming around,
And you, stark naked, on a low cane-bottomed chair
With vapour oozing off the new bread of your flesh?
Yours the winning kick, and cow-brown mud is still
Painted upon your powerful abraded frame.
Nico begins the singing, and the song,
In your own throat, felt like the ecstasy
Of ancient triumph at the river fords,
The frontier, or the debateable pass,
And the flattish beer sweet mead or great metheglins.

And do you remember that ecstatic
Lunacy, when Tonzer Price the medical
And you, wearing your top-coats inside out,
Heaving aloft your hats on cyclopean cabbage-stumps,
Paraded through the crowded city streets
In political burlesque? Jyder and friends
Follow, and proffer to amused, bewildered
Or affronted citizens, senseless
Handbills of slit newspaper. Marching ahead
With aldermanic gravity and aplomb, you hear
The bellowed idiocies of Steve and Jyder, who demand
Capital status for Cwmbwrla, the nationalisation
Of black women, and the state ownership of lineposts.

VOICE OF UNDESIRED MEMORY

Do you remember Nico dying, do you remember,
In that seaside cottage, with his winsome
Face gone skin and eager bone, and his
Crimson cough, and the animal
Glitter of his frightened eyes? Do you remember
Billy Handel, after his symphony,
Hands as though locked, arms impotent, his bones
Immovable upon his bed and slow
Blindness taking him before he died?

Do you remember Tonzer's hospital,
His cancer ward, the horror of the yellow tube
Draining from the mouth, the smell, the rotted nose,
Half the face devoured and painted purple black?
Do you remember how your soul cried out
In unavailing protest and in horror?
Do you remember in the mental hospital
The bearded old woman, melancholy,

63

With pale blue eyes, do you remember
All the world's ambition, all your pride,
Even your faith, arraigned in the despair
And heartbreak of that face? Do you remember?

VOICE OF MEMORY'S VARIANCE

Jake was a man of double deed
Who sowed his garden full of weed;
And when the weed began to grow
Jake had a heart as heavy as snow;
And when the snow began to fall
It sat like Death upon Jake's wall;
And when all walls began to crack
Dread was a rod upon Jake's back;
And when his back began to smart
Despair put a penknife in his heart;
And when Jake's heart begins to bleed
Then he'll be dead and dead indeed.

VOICE OF BLESSED MEMORY

Do you recall in holidays, the beach
Under metallic symbols of hung sun and moon,
With your children digging in the sand,
And the bay receiving into its hot lap
The burden of the tumbled sea. A few
Transparent clouds steam overhead, hauling
The spectral dragnet of their shade across
The curving shore. In the distance stands
The harvest-heaving headland, its base wrapped red
In rock against the outflung fires of the sun,
Fountaining into disruptive lace
The pounding sea. From time to time a gull,

Long, silent or snarling, above the sea-smoke,
Drawls at the corner of his airy periplus
And, pointing sideways his lit wing at the sea,
Pours down in swelling sunlight after it.
Seeing the children on the sand, the wistful boy
Brooding upon the rock, the gold-haired girl,
The dog barking, do you remember how
That flood of primaeval Bendigeidfranism
Filled your flesh with happiness and power,
So that you wished to clutch the rocks with either hand,
Sink your gigantic gulping mouth into the sea,
Gargle the Severn, shovel up the Tâf,
Spout into Stromboli smokes the Tywi's blue;
Back out the tides; roll up the oceans
Like a carpet for a sea-bed barn-dance;
Nail the big lip of a wave up over
Strumble Head; shawl all shores of Wales
With white Atlantic rock-wash? Do you remember
Your ring around Orion for shooting taws?
Do you remember kicking off the Polar Cap
Whose ice became your burning glass? Did you not bear
The orders of the Pleiades starry upon your shoulder?

VOICE OF UNDESIRED MEMORY

Do you remember, then, remembering,
Like a bitter regurgitation, shaven skulls,
Striped pariah clothing, squalor, madness and defeat
Encircled in barbed wire, glittering
And brand new? Hour after hour, standing
Silent and bareheaded in their sullen rows,
A thousand doomed endure the demoniac
Down-pouring of this sun. One turns his face
Sideways, as from the assault of great winds, or a blow,

Shudders and falls, his harsh voice anguished from
The torn throat of a crashing branch,
But unheeded there, his action commonplace,
His death beheld with the indifference
Of diurnal suffering.
                              Do you remember
The screeched agony of burning seamen
Fallen from their blazing tanker lighting
Up the sea, drowning in her fire,
The floating forest-blaze of flaring petrol
Spread upon the vast red acreage
Of ocean, while their shelled ship sank?
Do you remember how their screams broke out
From that seven times heated furnace, where walked
No comforter with the image of the Son of Man?

Do you remember how the shabby yellow men,
Their guns unslung, were vigilant beside
The deep ravine, watching at the brink
Your boy, their captive, loaded with digging tackle,
Crossing their crazy bamboo bridge, hesitant,
Bearing his body like the languid bones
Of anguished Lazarus, contending with despair,
Height's horror, and the lethargy of death?
O, Paraclete, redemptive hand of love,
O everlasting arms, why could no father's prayer
Impel you then to intermit the pallor of that face,
The torment of that heart, and of all flesh?

VOICE OF MEMORY'S VARIANCE

O where is the key of the keys of the kingdom?
Where is the key of the kingdom of pain?
Is the key drowned in the red of my heart's-blood?

Or is it buried deep in my brain?

Once, rose-milk and blood-red and pelting of perfume
Put a buzz in my pleasure like the passage of bees;
For beside the blue pane of the lake I was waiting
While silver light flitted like doves through the leaves.

Over velvet my lover walked at the lakeside;
The fish in blue water were silver as a vase,
And deep was the dome of our tree where the lip-lights
And gleam of her glance, had the soft flare of stars.

The hurt heart was soothed in the blossoms of sunshine.
The posies of nestling that cheeped, "Wake! Awake!"
And the blackbird, a bush-coal, drowned with their
                    vibrance
The growls of the thunders that broke from the lake.

They drowned with their music the thunders of groaning,
The weeping, the wailing that rose from the reeds.
We turned from our joy where the sun-laden branches
Bloomed in a milky-white blizzard of beads,

And saw from the lake side a haggard-eyed army,
The lonely, the laden, the lazars in rags,
The blind in their groping, the ribbed in their starving,
While the wolves and the ravens looked down from the
                    crags.

O, the sick and afflicted, the deep in defilement,
The silent in sorrow, the doomed in despair.
My lover turned pale at the wounds, and the coldness
Fallen heavy as lead on my hands was her hair.

For a tall sullen rider, still trailing green pond-weed,
Followed that army's woe over the land,
And, cursing my lover's compassion, shook blood
On her brow from the stump of his severed hand.

As though at a password. the cold of night enters.
The storm trails its hair over grey lake and plain;
A claw holds a glare in the boil of the tempest
And on branch and on bush falls the shawl of the rain.

O, the loud cries of torment that rose all around us,
The cries of mankind like the stricken beast.
Then I was a walker myself among mourners,
It pierced my breast like a gust of the east

To see, yellow-faced and red-eyed, my own lover
Weeping the tears of the sick and the slain;
By bushes the tempests had berried with brilliants
She walked like all flesh through the kingdom of pain.

Behind on his horse, the invincible rider;
But who is this One with the weeping crowd?
Who is it bears on his body the nail-marks,
The head of the blameless, bloody and bowed?

Where is the key of the keys of the kingdom?
Where is the key of the kingdom of pain?
Will the One find me the key that is hidden
Neither in heart's-blood nor buried in brain?

PART THREE

Mrs Owen: Why isn't Jake a Head?
Mrs Bowen: Why *isn't* he a Head?
Mrs Owen: He's too much of a churchman.
Mrs Bowen: He's too much of a red.
Mrs Cohen: He makes blots on his register and rubs them
out with bread!

Mrs Owen: Will Jake *ever* be a Head?
Mrs Bowen: He'll *never* be a Head.
Mrs Owen: Yet he knows those Latin poets.
Mrs Bowen: Knows the Greek ones too, it's said.
Mrs Cohen: He ought to know old Alderman Cadwaladar
instead!

Mrs Owen: Why isn't Jake a boss?
Mrs Bowen: Why *isn't* he a boss?
Mrs Owen: Some say he'd make a mess of it.
Mrs Bowen: Some say he's quite a loss.
Mrs Cohen: Some say as far as headships go he doesn't care
a toss.

Mr Owen: Jake's not fit to be a Head.
Mr Bowen: He's not at all well-bred.
Mr Owen: He lets the boys do anything.
Mr Bowen: Is he quite right in the head?
Mr Cohen: I heard those Baboon Terrace louts locked him
in his shed.

Mrs Owen: I can't see Jake a Head.
Mrs Bowen: He'll *never* be a Head.
Mrs Owen: He spites the other teachers.
Mrs Bowen: Once to spite the Head

He went home Monday playtime and spent the week
in bed.

Mr Owen: Why isn't Jake a boss?
Mr Bowen: As a Head he'd be imposs.
You never know what Jake will say
Once you get him cross.
Mr Cohen: He called those Baboon Terrace people muck
and moral dross.

Mrs Owen: Would Jake ever made a Head?
Mrs Bowen: An awful dance he's led.
They say he started nature study —
Now all his fish are dead —
The boys used marking ink and turned his aquarium
water red.

Mr Owen: Why isn't he a Head?
Mr Bowen: Jake will never be a Head.
Mr Owen: He's not a faithful churchman.
Mr Bowen: He's never been a red.
Mr Cohen: He's never joined the party club — is he quite
right in the head?

Mrs Owen: Why isn't Jake a boss?
Mrs Bowen: He'll never be a boss.
Mrs Owen: They say that every day in school
He takes a little doss.
Mrs Cohen: But no-one can call him the rolling stone that
never gathers moss.

Rees Art: After all these years Jake's bound to regard
his teaching with abhorrence.
Preece Chem: Why didn't he start to write sexy books

like that poet D.H. Lawrence
Who began, like Jake, in the Band of Hope,
        but rose above his station
By composing books with dirty talk
        about high-toned fornication?
Thos. French: Or why not follow Mallarmé, whose poems
        he goes on learning
When he hardly knows if murder is meant
        or only a cart-wheel turning?
Jones Latin: Jake says though ambiguity is very much
        to his fancy
He fears the Frenchman's line would mean —
        sharing a dentist's doxy!

Morgan Maths: Why doesn't he write like Milton, then,
        Tractates on Education,
His rhythms concern the fitting a man
        for any job in the nation?
Parry English: One thing he lacks — those Phillips boys —
        there's no-one upon whose breeches
He can dithyramb his rhythms out
        and yet ignore the screeches.
Preece Chem: Then what about that James Joyce man —
        they say he too was a teacher
Like Milton, Lawrence and Mallarmé —
        couldn't Jake think up some feature
To put our school on the map of fame
        and get himself some glory?
Omnes: Reading the classics is one thing —
        writing's a different story.

JAKE

Here I stand, a middle-aged teacher,
Behind my moustache like a straw-haired Nietzsche.
All is vanity, I say with the Preacher.

Here I stand, a middle-aged master.
When my heart went to stone and my world to disaster
I repaired my glasses with surgical plaster.

Profile of Rose

Hair-bowed Rose, deep in lush grass of the river
Bank, watched through the crystal unflawed block of
Afternoon, broad waters of her tenth birthday
Under sunglare, bottomless ebony
Sheeted with green and shine, and elms black
Along the far brink, and the gold field
Beyond, a shallow dishful of buttercup
Liquor. The painted tin toy, Rose's first
Dragonfly, blue, brilliant, then, oh, glassy,
Rinked glittering above the lit blades.
    In his ironmonger's villa her
      Camphor-coated father, her silk-sashed frock,
      Her bed — and heaped tableful of presents.
Motherless Rose hugged her kissing Jinny.
Not destined for philosophy or verse
She cried a child's laugh at the river bend
When, on the shining flats of lawn-like water,
Flocks of full-grown swans. thirty or forty,
Floated their perfection into what was
Already perfect.

* * *

          In boarding school, where
Philosophy, in the brochure, was not
In any schoolroom, Rose, in love with
Interchangeable goodness, beauty, truth,
Loved also spiteful, ill-favoured and lying
Angela, who loved nobody.
          In the
Abandoned boathouse, gloomy by the lake,
Motherless Rose, with swerve-necked orphan Angela,
Found sanctuary for gush and cake, where the girls'

Foundling swan, beguiled by Jinny's sponge, floated
And, webbed, walked the floorboards.

                   After a summer
Quarrel, innocent repentant Rose,
Sobbing, creaked open the boathouse door,
Shooting into the gloom sunlight, a stream
Of bullets sprayed around the walls, and saw,
Hanging heavily from low boathouse rafters,
The head battered, the great bulk of bright-plumaged
Body turning, leaden in sudden gold
Nettings of watery sunlight, on a neck
Stretched rigid and blood-sodden from the knotted
Rudder-ropes, their swan! Dead, dead, dead! Putty-
Coloured Angela, eating, watched it revolve,
The bleeding snapped-off oar-stump beneath her foot.

The two eyes of the ironmonger's head,
And Jinny's, Rose, disgraced swan-slayer, was returned
Villa-ward, where, from her delirious bed,
She screamed, unremitting, for the truth, the truth.

                 ★   ★   ★

    Rose, her dress, amber and bee-barred, pelted
With sunlight and perfume, went on long, slim
And eager legs to the river, to tan-skinned Charles.
Charles's surface was very beautiful.

The doting ironmonger's agony
Over, he died rich.
                   All Rose thought black blazed
Holy and unearthly. The swans gathered

Swaggering, the paddle of a webbed foot flamed,
Fidgetting the water, a black elbow,
Wrinkled as a dowager's, broke the surface.
Charles, lying, leaned over, grazing upon her
Golden, cheek-brusher lashes, each one curved
In the long shape of the beautiful
Avocet's slim bill; eyes lobelia-gay
Blue; straight, immature, early catkin-
Yellow hair. "The flesh in agony, the hurt
Heart desolate with disbelief, will the arms
And plaid of your tenderness be warm
Always about me?" Lightly the daisies
Pelted her lids. Charles's words were broken
For her like the living bread of truth.
"Always, always. My Rose. They will, they will".

★ ★ ★

Shuffling old woman, loutish, her sick, fringe-string
Hair lank, her hat knitted, her black cardigan
A mass of darns, smiled, with her sewing mouser
On the shanty sill, at the rain, sinking
Round as onion-rings in the marsh, and death.

At night, the great swans thronged the darkness, crashing
Through high marsh mist, blinded, wings torn off
On wires, bleeding, stunned, and Rose watched the wide
Flock, defiled in marsh slime, drown.
                                        Beauty was
Beauty, truth was Angela's untruth; was
Lying Charles the flying hero; dead Jinny's
Whiskey-pipe in a good overcoat; her
Father's Charlie, fit only for the kitchen

Fire-back; Rose's Charles the cheat; Charles brutal;
Charles adulterous; Charles and beggary.
Truth was age and abandonment, the starry
Firmament above and the malignant
Growth within, and death; truth — the writhing head,
Deadlier than lies, whose tranquil stare is stone.

On wide muds under rain, the wings severed,
Lay the plunging swans. Night — and the shining marsh
Held in its upward glare the moon; and milky
Majestic thunder, the rhythmic boom of
Throbbing voyagers broke out, the ruthless night
Swans' moon-blanched arrogance, that shook the marsh
And the heart of Rose shaken with laughter.

Dawn Trees

Morning of cold green, grape and the golden
   Water candles, crystal in soft stars, and
The fragile bangle of a new moon's milk.

Sun lights the blue palm, rooted upon the
   Shores of her long blue pool of shadow.

Old man in mourning, his knee-bone crooked, bows
   Beneath his burden, green leaves and black wine.

Breeze stirs the olive, the great grey wrestler
   Hurls off his invisible adversary.

Now is the juniper's green breeze called joy.

Morning

On the night beach, quiet beside the blue
Bivouac of sea-wood, and fresh loaves, and the
Fish baking, the broken ghost, whose flesh burns
Blessing the dark bay and the still mast-light,
Shouts, 'Come'.
       A naked man on deck who heard
Also cockcrow, turning to the pebbles, sees
A dawn explode among the golden boats,
Pulls on his sea-plaid, leaps into the sea.

Wading the hoarfrost meadows of that fiord's
Daybreak, he, hungering fisherman, forgets
Cockcrow tears, dark noon, dead god, empty cave,
All those mountains of miraculous green
Light that swamped the landing-punt, and kneels,
Shivering, in a soaked blouse, eating by the
Blue blaze the sweet breakfast of forgiveness.

Y Ddraig Goch

The Red Dragon flies aloft, behind him burns
The vast thinned out flame of golden sunrise.
   The city floats up in silver. Venus spills on the sea.

The Red Dragon waves over the blue carapace of roofs.
Breakers of the sun's illumination enter through windows,
   They appear as gleaming scabs on rococo decorations.

The Red Dragon leaps up. Swallows are elegant stumbler
The golden string of the sun is dabbled in the bay.
   Why is there no dancing among the cancerous?

The Red Dragon heaves joyfully in the suburban summe
A disorder of golden chains in tangled silence loads the
      trees.
   Coal is no less intractable in the two-foot seams.

The Red Dragon waves on high; once a dawn fire of
      twigs,
The hot sun now glints like tin on the green lagoon.
   The old language only is heard from the sunburnt
      beachfuls.

The Red Dragon flies forward; every dawn dewdrop is a
      peacock.
The great gold sun floats awash in the bay. Only Welsh is
      exchanged
   On Sunday beaches hideous with shit and transistors.

The Red Dragon triumphs over the silver-backed smoke
Until the city is a cairn, the language of Llanrhaeadr and
      Pantycelyn
   Shall be used for the utterance of her cruelty, her
      banalities, her lies.

The Red Dragon leaps above the inherited goal.
Sunbeams, incandescent up to the shoulder, probe into
        darkened cells.
What cause has conscience not to render the dragon his
        coinage?

The Red Dragon leaps, his claws and belly-mail are
        black.
The prisoner stares at the glowing ingot of his sunbeam.
Why should not bombs bring the paradise of daffodils at
        nine a penny?

The Red Dragon leaps like a demented acrobat.
To the convicted his comrades are a meadow of green grass,
   He objects to their being eaten equally by goats and
        unicorns.

The Red Dragon flies in green rain falling cold.
The sweet land, tender and fruitful under the native foot,
   Has long been the property of random foreigners.

The Red Dragon flies over valleys for sale. The Welsh
Mountains, loveliest under the suns of heaven,
   Are the inheritance of generations of native expropriators

The Red Dragon flies on every building. How can we,
        like the bullet-
Spattering Mexican, kneel down and give a scooped up
   Handcupful of Welsh soil Zapata's kiss of ecstasy?

Bindweed

Suddenly the scent of bindweed in the warm lane
And the smoking sea of remembering him bursts open
  Upon its rocks, its snow-dust wets the sun.

The heavy scent of bindweed brings only sorrow.
Grey gull-flocks puffed over waves disintegrate like
                 gunsmoke.
  Storm-sodden crags are not colder than my heart.

Bindweed is the scent of heavy remembering.
Beyond the window — the great ocean in its bed.
  I am alone. In the past Gwynn was with me.

The scent of bindweed drifts like childhood remembered.
Meshed white on green is the great wave's polished incurve.
  Bullets that took Gwynn were already in flight.

Cruel the sweet scent of innocent bindweed.
Winds tear off the tide's skin in one brandished fleece.
  Gwynn died. Happiness is irrational.

Bindweed now in this lane, then in that sea-garden.
Waves everywhere throw anguished arms around rocks.
  The comforter in his comforting is not comforted.

Sweet bindweed was heavy in that August garden.
The grey sea stiffens and sinks to a slab of iron.
  How is it the heart dead at its quick can suffer?

Where All Were Good to Me, God Knows

Seeing the block of flats, I remember
The meadows under them, where Jones the Stoning's
Skewbald cart-horse would walk in sunshine
Camouflaged conspicuous as a tank,
Among the fluid swallows,
And the Jones' white-washed house,
And their long garden with the door in the wall,
In at which squat Russ and I floated and, through
Subaqueous gloom of their glass trees, out
On to their sunlit lawn, vast and glowing.
"Welcome, come in, my boy", said Mr Jones
— A shy man, he was never in the handshake
First to remit the pressure — adding
"zzz", when he saw there were two of us.
God bless much overfed, norfolk-suited,
Green-stockinged, yellow-booted Mr Jones
— Destined for his nest, must be, I thought, that fluff
Moustache — his high collar, his high colour
Glassy, tight over his shining head
The polished membrane of his tarry hair.
And his crippled Philip also, rowdiest
Hunchback goalie in the game — I remember
His brown hair-helmet (in sunlight the red
Gravy of sea-iron), his sad faces inked
On finger-nails, his nutmeg freckling,
The feel of crutch-pads warm from his armpits.

We played cards and ate apples,
While sweating Mr Jones, dumb talker,
Witty listener, sat watching us before
His red bed of flat sun-gulper tulips,
And the sun-soaked wall where deep udders
Of shadow hung down darkening the brickwork —
Beaming, his fat hand nursing his fat fist.

A raft of starlings exploded off the grass,
A full thrush hopped heavily with long
Kangaroo hops down the lawn and slowly
Mrs Jones followed, long-frocked from the dazzling house.
God bless his beautiful Mrs Jones also,
Her drake-head-green gown, her broad-brimmed hat, her
                cool
Face gold, radiant in lawn-reflected amber,
Her smile a mirror in which I smiled to see
Myself always clever, beautiful and good,
And before which off-white-handed Russ blushed
Into his shirt, and his aitches were the aitches,
Soon, of a boy who never sounded aitches.
    Mr Jones's face turned sharp out of shadow
Towards her, smiling, and some long curled tendril,
Some hot nostril hair, suddenly lit up red,
Glowed in sunlight like a burning filament.

    All are dead, Jones the Stoning, Mrs Jones,
Philip, Russ, the charm, the tenderness, the glow.
Evening drops a vast sun into sunset
Where it smoulders swollen, boiling behind
The flats — once the great cart-horses pounded on
Pavings of those night-fall-slated meadows,
Where grey Danter, too, the Jones's pig-headed
Pony stood asleep beneath the burnt-out tree.
God bless beautiful flats also, I suppose.
Lights go on in windows. People live in them
And great stars flash among vanished branches
And night-owls call from elms no longer there.

Goodbye, What Were You?

At the voice of the mother on a warm hearth,
　　Dark and firelit, where the hobbed kettle crinkled
In the creak and shudder of the rained-on window,
　　This world had its beginning
And was here redeemed.

All in that kitchen's warmth, that mother's glow,
　　Was blessèd, nothing was abandoned.
There God's boy was born, loving, by lantern light,
　　His church built of the breathing of cattle;
Before nightfall all lost in prowling woods were home;
　　To the dying in cactus land a hand came full of rain;
Here a child wept repentant into a Father's breast,
　　Warm for his childish tears, not bright with stars,
Or filled with his suffering that mother's arms
　　And in the shawls of her prayers and kisses slept.

In the kitchen shadow and flicker and warmth,
　　And the deafening storm, thickening hair by hair
Its blinding pelt of tempest on the window panes.

Images of Light and Darkness

Passing the suburb's wintry sea-fence, when a gale
    Shrieked a continent's disasters plastered
Across papered pig-wire, I sighted, high, calm
    Above the bay, black bird-flocks, curved like combers,
Homing purposefully for the mountain pass.
    That unfaltering flesh stood me in the storm
Of my exile, alone, the homeless part anguished
    In the cold chink of put-out milk bottles.
Now there is never going indoors, to comforting
    Warmth; there too, even in musky fragrance of applewood
Burning, only the endless gale against the windows,
    The lashed glass drenched, the shriek of the beach's
Vegetation tumbled, earth's shrill anguish
    Unassuaged, a thundering out of stars,
Heavenly sapphires, gold-filled gulphs, apple-green
    Sea-pools remembered as tenderly luminous.

On cream hills in the sun, leopards and hibiscus
    Burned like bonfires. Her purple shadow with the
Golden holes lay spread beneath the carob tree,
    Her leaves pushed by the river breeze, and some white
Epiphany moved exultant in the flamy fields.
    Beside that Tâf, its golden skin twitching
Under flies, children, we prayed, our sunlit flesh
    Pelted with shadows of white alighting doves;
While over Jordan, distant in the field, I watched
    The farmer's fire, building from fragile smokes
Pavilions of blue glass, I heard the cold-maned
    Ponies wild among our windy daffodils;
And where darkness lay upon the deep, where snow-footed
    To the fishing boats, the towering Light trod,
Vestured in torrid purple, like creation,
    I rushed my love upon the sea, my foot could not go
        through.

Thunder breaks from the waves, the melted windows
  Run down in rain. Somewhere, o where, is advent,
Spring, for thrushes, far out on their boughs,
  To whistle nearer the threshold; when with death,
Indifference, disenchantment, the loving ends,
  Comforting spring to proffer honeysuckle's clawful
Of perfume, black branches brilliant under amber buds,
  And water-buds, and sweet swoops of heavy blackbirds.
Spring, glimpsed across our midnight frontier like
  The cigarette glow of some dubious redeemer,
Where is your abidance? You, wayward and fragile,
  In this rending wind black from the slaughter of
Towering mud-tufted beaches, the shattered tillage,
  Scabbed armies of skeletons — you, lovely in your
            drench
Of flower-flesh, pure white, epiphanal, veined with
  Silver, flushed fish-pink, clotted, golden and blood-
      smudged.

War and Peace

Under the vast burning-glass of the Second
World War's hatred, I walked dying down
Bridge Street, Pontypridd, and flung out suddenly

Wide wings, are they, soaring in some torrid gyre —
Great boughs, exultant, naked in the gale —
This glow, is it rosier than the low sun's
Firelight, jammed ruby in autumn sumacs —
Coiled, am I, in the hot armpit of the hills,
Warming my orange wampum in your rays?

Through the black cloud's roof of agony, your rigid
Beams fell vertical and golden with the sheen
Of oil, fruitful upon my deserts, your broken
Milk bled, slaking the huge suck of my roots.

What happened was little enough like this.
But how could I, frightened and confused, present,
Even to those who believe and speak
The language, the meaning of *tangnefedd Duw?*

Another Country

The young sycamore puts out new slender stems
    Among bomb-site willowherb and white-limed
Masonry; her wax buds break, each long bead or pod,
    Pinkish, packed with its tight toad's hand of leaf,
Opens in fragile emerald, but soft;
    Her leaves turn, soon, solid bronze, opaque
In sunshine, metallic, sharply incised,
    But breathing, tender, alive and beautiful.

The children have put a rope around her neck.

From my upstairs schoolroom window once I watched
    The child run from his empty sun-baked yard
And cross the meadow, making for the dark woods.
    Somewhere upon that path, that universe's
Longest voyage, from heart to heart, I stand lost,
    Love's road leads back, always, here, journeys back
Towards this other mystery of my self,
    While the child moves on beyond, exultant
And incommunicable through his dark trees —
    Woods of untarnished images, perceptions
Like thunderclaps, chimeras, symbols,
    Passion, terror, ecstasy, despair.

O dark impenetrable forest,
    Over whose frontiers, for what strange rituals,
Propitiation, sacrifice perhaps,
    Unfathomable ceremonials of their guilt
And innocence, do the children lead
    The doomed beauty of this bursting sycamore?

The Common Path

On one side the hedge, on the other the brook:
    Each afternoon I, unnoticed, passed
The middle-aged schoolmistress, grey-haired,
    Gay, loving, who went home along the path.

That spring she walked briskly, carrying her bag
    With the long ledger, the ruler, the catkin twigs,
Two excited little girls from her class
    Chattering around their smiling teacher.

Summer returned, each day then she approached slowly,
    Alone, wholly absorbed, as though in defeat
Between water and hazels, her eyes heedless,
    Her grey face deeply cast down. Could it be
Grief at the great universal agony had begun
    To feed upon her heart — war, imbecility,
Old age, starving, children's deaths, deformities?
    I, free, white, gentile, born neither
Dwarf nor idiot, passed her by, drawing in
    The skirts of my satisfaction, on the other side.

One day, at the last instant of our passing,
    She became, suddenly, aware of me
And, as her withdrawn glance met my eyes,
    Her whole face kindled into life, I heard
From large brown eyes a blare of terror, anguished
    Supplication, her cry of doom, death, despair.
And in the warmth of that path's sunshine
    And of my small and manageable success
I felt at once repelled, affronted by her suffering,
    The naked shamelessness of that wild despair.

Troubled, I avoided the common until I heard
    Soon, very soon, the schoolmistress, not from

Any agony of remote and universal suffering
    Or unendurable grief for others, but
Private, middle-aged, rectal cancer, was dead.

What I remember, and in twenty years have
    Never expiated, is that my impatience,
That one glance of my intolerance,
    Rejected her, and so rejected all
The sufferings of wars, imprisonments,
    Deformities, starvation, idiocy, old age —
Because fortune, sunlight, meaningless success,
    Comforted an instant what must not be comforted.

Nant Ceri

Blessèd were those Bowens who saw all this — viz,
    Dawn's sort of rosin glow, then the sun's red-gold
    Mountain, floating up through green, a dazzle
    In windows distant from this window; masses
    Of garden azaleas bloom plum-blue, porcelain,
    Apricot, or their liquor, from emerald
    Fogs under the iron pear boughs, glows ruby
    Like jewels or lit wine; the long-tailed mountain pony,
    Milky, saddled with morning silver, wax-white
    On fire-green turf her unshod hooves, munches
    In this hush of mountains her black rug
    Of shadow; breeze blows the green grass blaze glossy
    And bends, bows into a gentle curve, the children's
    Rope, hung from branches of the flashing orchards;
    A green moon too clouds milky as sea-glass —
Blessèd were those Bowens who saw all this
For three lifetimes and believed in God.

You, Taliesin

You, Taliesin, in the great *Addwynau*
  Of your elaborate praise,
Called over a hundred things beautiful —
  Long-maned stallions at stud,
    Silver bracelets and necklaces,
      The age of innocence,
        Charlock in young corn.

I ought perhaps to feel a little shame-faced
  At bringing into my own droned fragment of celebration
Such words and ideas as —
  Beautiful the sawn-off girder seen in the Valleys,
    Rusty, sticking sun-plastered out of the
    coke-ovens' brickwork;
Or, beautiful the staring old collier,
  Silent by the coal fire, too old,
    His hands on his knees,
      Cared-for and yet abandoned;
Or, beautiful the drab mining town,
  Its roofs fishskin under endless drizzle,
Where, young, I saw that politics
  Was about power, and people, and dreams.

But beautiful to me also the sea,
  Which no doubt you intended to praise
Although you didn't;
  Beautiful to watch her waters hurled,
A struggling mass, into a corner of the rocks;
  Or to see her great waves crawling their whitewash
Up the plastered cliff —
  Withdrawing, she hangs delicately
Along the ledges of the black rock-wall
  The milky vines of her foam.

Beautiful the sky, too, as you describe it,
    The hot sun high at mid-day, or glowing large at his
                setting;
And the smouldering of his long beams in the sultry
                afternoons
    His shafts leaning up off the meadows, rigid into the
                summer thunder-clouds,
Entering into some great funnel opening in those heavens,
Sloping up in thick bundles of rods, golden and
    vaporous, or flat, sliced into oblique sheets
    of radiant whale-bone, or sombrely lined,
    diagonal, smoky, with the black slant of
    brilliant rigging.

Beautiful the night sky also,
    The clouds blown about gusty as woodsmoke
Before the beam of the moon's open doorway;
    Beautiful in some tranquil nightfall of autumn
A large wet star.

You, Taliesin, you did not proclaim —
    Any more than that the sea is beautiful —
Beautiful to be free, to be forgiven, to create.
    I sense your understanding, your expert concurrence.

Dafydd's Seagull and the West Wind

DAFYDD'S SEAGULL ADDRESSES HIM

Sir, after all that sweet cod,
The soft soap and the maldod —
Moon-matcher, comber-lily,
Snow-semblanced nun of the sea! —
You made me, master, say yes,
And try to find her fortress.
But rather, since White-as-pith
Lived miles from Aberystwyth,
And you wanted an answer
In a flash, hot-hearted sir,
I passed on your passion's cry
*To the wind, my sub-*llatai,
My diving lover, my date,
My moth-soft-breathing playmate,
My perfume-picker, my tall
Tree-shudderer of crystal.

HIS SEAGULL ADDRESSES THE WIND

Wind, why could you not bring back
Some message for this maniac,
Some sign from that paragon
Up there beyond Pumlumon,
Some signal, relenting word?
Why leave his pleas unanswered?

Wind, my wings in ton-up dives
Buzzed on your barbs like beehives;
I felt on my taut midriff
And pinion-bones your soft biff,
As your back bronchoed the rings

96

Of my boisterous white buckings.
Contentious, and me a bridge,
Your reckless torrent — courage! —
Wrecked me, your blood-loud roarings
Crashed both arches of my wings.

Up sun-sloshed slopes your breath blows
A pilgrimage of shadows,
And, crowding above those stains,
White clouds, homers to mountains,
Their slow groping hands sightless,
You shepherd through the green press
Of peaks — you guide soft-fingered
Summit-fumblers, your blind herd.

Corn-ears clash, your brushing wings
Rouse their concerted peckings,
And sweep that albino sea
Black, the battling tall barley.

You, roaring forest-ghost, purr,
Roosting on boughs; your whisper,
In the jungle's throat, becomes
A rugger-roar of welcomes.
You sigh trees-full of pendant
Catkin-fringes in a slant,
Scattering sycamore keys
And ripe fire-blooms of poppies.

My wild wind, my gruff bellows,
Spoiler and boiler of boughs,
Why have you left me to face
Alone this mouth of menace?
Come, wind, from sodden mountains,

Drum down on him drenching rains,
Or else embrace his love-glow
Decked in your sea-coat of snow.

Henffych, Dafydd

Rain-bombed under boughs, I crouch
By brown housebricks in ruins.
Jewels on gossamer, gems,
A spider's net-full, glazes
With glassy lace of diamonds
The ruin's smashed window-pane —
Sparkling sea-mist's insignia,
Rain's jewelry, encrusted brooch,
Lustre of fiery crystals
Glittering in first-water gems,
Brilliants minute as mousemilk,
Diamonds glowing in long rows.

You, Dafydd, *eos Dyfed*,
To me spinner, maker, more,
Rain-finery's fisherman,
Netter of downpour's glitter.

Which side, Dafydd, did you serve,
If either? The English king's,
Like so many of your clan?
Were you some Baudelaire, skilled bard,
Indifferent agitator?
Did you glimpse, as Iolo once,
Culture's brutal nourishing,
Welshmen broken on Welsh land?
You, poet of love's contretemps,
Did you see *taeog*'s toiling,
Gross, sustaining foam-brows' grace,
Burnishing their broom-yellow?

I first read your words dazzled,
Heart's skin suddenly too small,
Merthyr's hair shirt forgotten
And that blade through my rib-cage.

In ecstasy, despairing,
A seablue road through Dyfed
I walked, the wind-current's bed.
A sea-gull, scarcely moving
Majestic sun-mantled wings,
Floated that air-flood's surface,
The turn of her perfect head
Imperious and indifferent.
"God, why shall I never show
One thing, anything, as sweet
(Beauty's adroit creators)
As her moving's mastery,
As yours of the bright image?"

Dafydd, I, one more croaker,
Admirer and lamentor,
Brought you once my clumsy songs.
I observed your moon's changes —
"Curved, yellow as candle-flame";
"White gleam your silver kingdoms";
"Ghostly, pale, demented moon,
You haunt Hafren's blue noon sky";
"You float towards black cloud-banks
The shine of your polished keel".
Standing in your gale I watched
A shouting wind — "With one hand
You drag off by the hair clouds
Clawing at the Beacons' scowl";
Heard too the wind's tiny whine —
"Your note sad through the conch-hole
Of the smallest blown snail-shell".
Lit by your dawn suns I saw
The young birch of the shaved lawn —
"You gather your dark shadow

Over green grass towards you,
A dragging train of black lace.
You hang it over your arm".

From these crude fragments you turn,
Indulgent and indifferent,
Widening your grin — clown's, *prifardd*'s —
On the girls, the golden wives,
The devastating daughters.

Bright sun breaks over white gulls;
Rain burns in the jewelled webs;
With dancer's delicacy
The spider paws the brickwork,
Gathering the brown ruined wall.

Swifts

Shut-winged fish, brown as mushroom,
The sweet, hedge-hurdling swifts, zoom
Over waterfalls of wind.
I salute all those lick-finned,
Dusky-bladed air-cutters.
Could you weave words as taut, sirs,
As those swifts', great cywydd kings,
Swart basketry of swoopings?

Friends and Falls

I think, of many living friends,
Which would I fancy standing here
Most, at this rowdy waterfall
And in this golden evening light —
Wynn-Jim, or Jack, or Morris John?

The sunlit view beyond the gorge
Hangs bright and bat-like in the pool
Paved luminous and blue with sky;
The stagy glare illuminates
Those glassy waters, radiant boughs,
Each glowing green upended beech,
The trunks of birches, plunging down
Their searching necks like sunlit swans,
Solidified in evening glow
Of the pool's black solidity,
As, brilliant in the mind of Wynn
My friend, poor chap, the thoughts stand forth
Reflected clear, but upside down.

The gorge's sunless sides are slabs
Of vast black rocks, wall-papered wet
With sludge-green pricy-looking moss;
The pool's glass bends across its lip
In one thick shiny plastic sheet,
Transparent, outward-curving, cold,
An always-slamming bread-bin lid
That plunges, deafening, greeny cream,
In the stunned torrents of the gorge,
Milky carnation, ideal suds,
From which the unsunned salmon blast
Bright metals of their rocketry.
I love you, Jack, but you seem more
Tractatus theologico-

Politicus, sometimes, than friend;
I am so shrieked at, thundered on,
Only my obmutescence keeps
Peace between cataract and friend.

Below the gorge the flattened foam
Sprawls wide its Celtic lettering,
Its intricate white capitals
Smooth on the river's placid ale.
If you, dead Morris, gentle friend,
Broke out from your oblivion and
Assumed this evening's blinding glow —
Not with your strolling to disturb
Those sparrows bathing in the dust
I know I'd see you walking wide.

Crossing the Bars

Tall, windy Tennyson would sometimes growl his way
    Down to the village, Haslemere, to fetch his post,
Poetic in his wide-awake and long black cloak.
    Once, on the road, he met the village boy whose job
Was bringing telegrams to Aldworth House, the Bard's
    Swanky new mansion. "Telegram for you, please, Sir",
The kid said, bowing, handing up the envelope.
    Despite posh family, fancy d'Eyncourts and that,
And he himself a Peer — O.K., a baron only,
    First, too, but what can you expect from poetry? —
Spoilt, flattered Tennyson, rugged too frequently
    And rather short on tact, remembered. "Boy", he
            boomed
Down, "don't hand that thing to me here. Let's walk
            together
    Back a bit, to touch the milestone — then you can claim
The tuppence extra for your job. Come on". They did.
    One of the Laureate's nicer lyrics, I always think.

At the Window

Let me avoid that gazing-stock, for God's sake,
Always, in our village, at best my greeting be
Meagre or perfunctory of such
Grotesque failure, limping unseeing against
The sunlight's militancy across the Square,
Or down our lane, his bitch, his half-blind amber
Cocker leading him, and from the frayed
Pocket of his shroud-like overcoat fresh butcher's
Meat, perhaps, and newsprint, dangling.
But yet, always, even in such unutterable
Banality as our village Square's, or lane's,
His failure and aloneness speak, always, great truth.

Now, dawdling and bemused, he stares towards
My window through my thrusting birches,
Their metals white among their lacy smokes.
Eyes, blank in that large-featured face of solid bone,
See nothing, see but intrigue, see only treachery.
I can recall his distant cottage and its windows,
Night after night lit, late and early, that grave where
Glory and great music finished, both, for him.
Despite the silenced clocks, the padded studio,
Equipment, instruments, pianos, the great grand;
Despite two sullen daughters, now dead, neglected,
The scandal of that silent second wife
Sacrificed, long since insane; despite
Demoniac dedication, despite the early
Reputation that came thundering briefly
Through his cottage letterbox — the change
Of modes, of cadences, brought for him
Neglect, obscurity, despair, brought silence,
The crazed wanderings, the slit wrists.

He shuffles on, his sea-grey greatcoat ankle-length,
Hatless, the uncut locks of musical hair
White above the stoop and rubber hump; those strange
Hands, black backs and monkey-pink palms that,
He drones, "Still wear the golden glove of harmony";
On to his cottage and the shrill torment
Of his sister's vigilance and mockery.
Waking in dawn's darkness, when the perceptions
Of the old are at their brightest and most
Bitter, I think of him, and the whole world's
Failures, whose wounds, whose tears, thrust us again
Back into the anguish of our own despairs.

Birch

The young birch models in the green breeze
    The fluttering laciness of her leafy dress.
The sun's fireplace grows cold, winter comes —
    On the lawn now, alone, without a silk stitch on,
She stands each night entangling stars.
    Soon, delicately, in darkness, the snow falls;
Once more is her silver dressed in whiteness,
    In the brilliance of the milky openwork,
And in that morning splendour, radiant
    Beside the pool of the heart's troubled waters,
The lovely slut strips naked again.

Remembering Mari

Below the ward's darkening window
   I kiss the old inflamed cheek,
Hard, glassy, chill to my lips,
   And see a young woman at dusk walk
From the dark farmhouse, beside the hedge,
   While summer lightning flickers.
She crosses with the child the hill field's gloom,
   Between them the earthenware pitcher —
They bear now no thought, no knowledge,
   Of body's bliss, the agony, the squalor.
The stars burn low over the earth,
   We skirt the dark rick of kindling,
The pony's gold looms from the alders.
   Down at the sloping end of the grass
We reach the well's chill waters,
   We bury our cream under a dish of stars.
At the window the lightning's vein throbs agonised
   In the flesh of darkness, as I kiss, despairing,
For the last time, the crimson, stone-cold cheek.

Spring Bush

Fine twig, not more slender, more delicate, more dark,
       the undipped shank
Of the wading water-bird, and spread along
       its thong-like length,
Light, fragile, a scattering of golden blossoms —
       beautiful in sunlight
Lightning-yellow alighting blooms, like
       four-winged twin imagos,
Flowers whose glow is gold, petals beaked bright
       with cut emeralds;
They float out, gold finery along slenderness,
       each flamy bloom
A yellow flare, a brilliance, jewelled lures
       as of transcendental fishflies.

If we had made one such, one twig, one would say,
"Preserve it for ever. Do not touch.
Bring the glass dome and the alarm system.
Such golden loveliness is our fragile heritage".

From the pocket of some over-prodigal, shower,
       as in golden-pelted fiestas,
Ten thousand billion such, gold blooms chucked
       thick covering park grasses,
Untold gold in mounds clogging the gutters
       of his grieving children,
Falling flowery on our silent streets — sadder,
       more deathly
And fuller than we know — pelting past
       despairing windows —
There it sits helplessly, the horror
       of the ring of idiots —
Are golden snowdrifts showered on agonies
       of tornado-flattened towns,

On steps of some shell-shattered chancellery
    are spread in deep gold carpetings
Where among the silences an ignorant dead girl
    sobs, giving her dead child suck.

And here upon each branch, each varnished arm
    thrust out, naked, willowy,
The blossoms cluster in thousands, throng here yellow
    and bee-swarm dense, each bough's skin
Invisible beneath thick crusts of golden petals,
    each branch broadly bangled
With yellow radiance, with deep bracelets
    of honeyed flower-scabs,
With clustering jewelry of golden wings,
    with spiky light of roughened gold.

Here I watch the sad, the marvellous, the gold-
    pelted agony, transient
Golden elegance and long-suffering in great
    mid-day gold of sunlight,
I watch gold and know agonised endurance
    stretching out to touch.

Jakey crosses the School Pitch

Black-headed gulls, massed solid as a bus,
Flock in the ruins of poor Jakey's head,
Black-eyed with button-glass, grey-mantled, lean.
One lands and floats the thick green sea
Of school field grasses, all summer feathers snow,
Her tail forks sooty, thinking herself in paradise,
And Jakey too, sunning themselves off Wharley Point,
Afloat upon the ocean's lifting lid,
Some shiny, wet, green, metal sheet, breaking in foam
Against the far-off wardrobes of the summer cliffs.

The sun enters the field, borne dripping underneath
An elm's arm, lighting up the blown newsaper's
Imperious page that, rising, thinks itself majestic
Snow-white swan, perhaps, or greater blackback,
Ruthless on vast bent blades, and Jakey smiles to watch —
It glows for him among the sky's unseen huzzars,
Although no more, alas, than yesterday's *Express*
That, falling, plasters the hedge. Jakey is doomed.
Jakey has bright perceptions, but sad thoughts;
He has experienced every flight of certainty.

Backed by a square of sky's blue cardboard,
The husband crouches down in full white overalls,
Alone and humped and grumpy on the crossbar,
On the dirty rugger posts. A seabird, silent, he will
Never utter a sweet song. He knows the anarchic ocean
And has given up all hope. There are no gifts,
But bribes and payments only, no consummation, no
Finality, no triumphs — each the bleak
Beginning of some new defeat. His tears flow
With Jakey's. He wipes his eye with his ankle.

Superior

When I was in the grammar school I used to love
The Morris girls, all three of them, although
The youngest was my senior by, maybe,
Ten years. The lovely thing about them was,
They were so superior — they had
That natural, unquestioned, unproclaimed
Superiority, they just knew, always,
That they were superior, and that was that. Beyond
Our little town park — with fountain, pond and
                bandstand —
Above our rigid terraces, they had their tall,
White-and-yellow villa, old-fashioned, nice,
(Their dada was some sort of registrar),
Not seedy-posh, not like those flashy Sharkey
Richardses, who had a butler for a bit,
And half a race-horse, but no-one ever thought
Of that lot as superior. (The dad there was
A bookie, bandy, bald, with short brown teeth).
I called up at the Richards' villa once —
The old rectory really, with them become half farm,
But 'our disorderly house' to those three
Knowing, crazy Richards girls — to see Dai Adrian,
The son, my friend, who'd just been sacked from
                Cambridge
— Some daft drunk jape that crashed his father's
Second-hand Rolls Royce — and watched the sisters
Shove an ailing short-horn mooing up their wide
Front steps, into their sitting room, placarding
With a steaming poultice its gigantic udder, and Dai,
Down on his knees in that god-awful room,
Stark naked, painting the skirting puce,
While the beast messed plentifully on the mat
And then collapsed dead in the fireplace.
The Morris girls were always beautifully dressed

(Not beautiful themselves though, though none were
            prettier)
Their glittering dark elegance silken across
Our square, never flamboyant, never spectacular,
But always in the stunning best of taste.
And they were never snobbish either, not reserved —
The three were much too nice for that — they were
Superior only, always charming, delicate,
Assured and superior.
                    The only time
I ever spoke to them, really spoke, was on
My fourteenth birthday party visit to our theatre;
My friends and I happened to sit next to them; they talked
To me about the actors and the play, and they knew,
They said, Ivor, my older cousin, and Miss Mari Ann
Passed their box of chocolates round my guests and me.

I used, later, to see them on their way to church
On Sunday mornings, when they always glanced, bowed,
Smiled, the three, walking our high street pavement
In a swish of silk, leaving a powerful fresh scent behind.

The tallest one, Miss Enid Oliver,
Had thick, white-golden hair, big eyes of baby-blue
And lovely long silk legs. She left our town,
Married to some land-agent chap, tweedy, gross,
His vast and sullen face a mauvish crimson,
Who used, aloof, to ride his coal-black hunter through
Our square and lived out in the sort of country place
The lord-lieutenants come from — and before
A year was out she'd stuck a bread-knife twice
Up to the bone hilt in his groin. Soon, soon,
She was dead, mad, in jail. Miss Judy was
The smallest one, a ballet dancer, so they said,

Powdered, white-faced, petite, with glittering made-up
                eyes.
She too left town. When she returned she bared her neck
One night and laid it on our local railway line,
Waited, and the bogeys of our colliers' train
Sliced her head off. Nightly for years Miss Mari Ann,
The middle one, proclaimed her lonely presence
By her lighted candle in their crumbling villa,
Alone, unwashed, her stockings down, unfed,
Old early and neglected in the stink and solace of
Her twenty cats, her rows of whisky bottles.

About these three, to whom I gave such
Boyish devotion, this I heard years later from
My wise superior Mam, who understood, well,
The perils of all sweet superiority.

Bathsheba

A stray beam rainbows the mirror bevel;
 Gown, bangles, gleam on our bed;
Bolt up the windows of your joy,
 David, on my dead —

Silence that thud of passing drums
 To the pulse of blood or clock;
Turn against pity your iron key
 Cold in your palace lock;

Look, first, look down at my captain's funeral
 Choking the sullen street —
Close, close our bedroom shutters — lock
 Out that murderous beat.

Thunders your blood against my flesh,
 Drums thunder out in the glare;
Louder the feet of my child's burial
 Thunder, descending your stair.

Thanks to John

(for his nice radio programme)

This, dear John, just means I am
Delighted with the programme.
How did you get that great mass
Of stuff down to the compass
Of half an hour? — though time here,
(For *this* enchanted listener),
A green thought in a green shade
Was, not second or decade.

Herbert, too, deserves my praise
For his recording forays,
First to Gwyn's Aberystwyth,
Then to that other home of myth,
Llanstephan, loved by Dylan;
And of course to Penylan.

I've never heard my poems
Sound more like poetic gems
Than when — in Darren's velvet —
Words, style and emotion met.

But as the tape wound onwards
Most of all I loved your words,
John, — nothing heard is sweeter
To the hopeful poet's ear
Than voice of peer, poet, friend,
Subscribing to that legend
That each writer must cherish
Of himself, be it but wish
Only, no more based on truth
Than an advert for vermouth.
Dear John, I can't hope to say

How much I enjoyed Friday,
Listening to tapes recalling
So many a forgotten thing,
And your voice unerringly
Praising what sounds good to me.
And this brings me to my cue
To say, John, "Thank you. Thank you".
And may no-one bend that bond
Between me and John Ormond.

After the Sermon

Amen. Sunday morning sunshine and some stackyard's
    Fragrance flood in at the open chapel doors;
The village worshippers stand silent, bowed, their thoughts
    Groping again among their handbags, glasses, gloves;
The hoarse harmonium's pumped out benediction dies
    And that sunlit Saron's boyish organist,
A grin bright on his burnt farm face, swivels
    Across his bench and, on the greek-key bordered
Oilcloth of the aisle, drops to his knee,
    His arms outspread. His wife, tall in the doorway,
Stands vexed and smiling in the dazzle, lowering
    Their baby daughter's fidgeting boots down
To the brown oilcloth, and releases her.

The child bolts off in mindless ecstasy,
    Along that rowdy aisle, heedless, blissful, intense,
And plunges, clinging, into her father's arms.
    "'*Nhad. 'Nhad. 'Nhad*".

Perfect, that moment of his embracing her.

Perfect, when men and women, at that trivial end,
    Seeing it, were swept perhaps back into some great
Engulphing ecstasy of love again, some warm remembered
                arms
    Of flesh, mother's, lover's, friend's; and those, the few,
Guiltless a moment and redeemed, did they feel,
    Beyond the dazzle and the fragrance and the love,
At that embrace, about their fleeting blessedness,
    The sunlit comfort of the cold eternal arms?

Bethania

I bring the wrinkled workman, risen from the dead,
To park gates, he wearing cap and muffler, winter
Overcoat; dumb there he stands, staring, at peace;
Out of the tomb came lacerated belly, bandaged pipe
And pipe-cough, and long and gluttonous
           Engulphing stare.

Crows burn, bright as pheasants, in the shrubs;
Over high levels of the park's grey rocks
Hang sunlit beards of straight-lipped waterfalls,
Tall and whitewashed, they fall and are blessed;
A gaggle of grey geese, huddled close in the long
Glitter of his gaze, crank their rusty gear of rafts,
Loud and discordant, across the boat-pond.
His Bethany burns in silent joy, is brilliant
With benediction, fragrant, ablaze and unconsumed —
Death was not yet for him, not yet. A ball
Is slogged; exultant breeze leans
In regattas of flying children; under dark
Trees pools of burning sunlight smoulder
           Green on blinding grass.

Death was not yet, grave linens, face-cloth,
Death's stink not yet to be; beside him at the warm
Black bars I watch and share tranquility,
A visionary peace possesses him, a brooding joy,
His chrism of tears and quietness, between grey gate-stones
           And the iron bars.

Remembering Alcwyn

Defenceless, unprepared, I heard that stranger read,
Indifferent, from memorial chapel bronze,
The silenced name, and so recall the vast
Timeless destruction of one single death.

"Take these to Alcwyn on your way to school".
The time approaches Christmas, 1917. I go
Eagerly to see my soldier cousin,
Home on leave from France, who used
To take me in their high-wheeled yellow trap
Delivering their cloth, their bolts of tweed,
Galloping their brown-bread pony up the mountain roads,
Jeering at the slow-coach milkmen's horses and the coal-car
Whistling, shouting, "Get up, Kronje, boy,
Get up, Kronjooter", making us laugh, the stiff
Wind shining carrot in his curls; and sat
By me in chapel, moulding in sermon time
From toffee wrappers, fragile paper chalices,
And at his call-up gave his fret-saw, cork-grips,
Gyroscope to me. I knock at their little woollen
Factory's side door. Instantly my uncle opens, tries,
Sweet man, his bloodless face without all consolation,
Cold, to smile his customary wrinkled smile.
I hold out the cardboard box of Welsh-cakes.
"Mam said, 'for Alcwyn' ". "Come in", he mutters, though
He seems now hardly to notice me. We walk on
Through their gloomy workroom passages
Into the half-dark kitchen's warmth. Alcwyn,
The white-faced boy, shrunk in his bulging khaki
Greatcoat, his soldier's brass-badged khaki cap
Monstrous on his cropped red hair,
Sits at the breakfast table, silent, frozen,
Stern, perhaps trying to eat something. Black-shawled
Beside the kitchen range, hostile and resentful, holding

Brass tongs and coal tin, his mother, through
Thick glasses peers round at me, but from the anguish
Of that bitter spirit's torture chamber, no words,
And, ending an endless silence, the kitchen
Wall-clock strikes nine. Alcwyn rises, stands mute,
Apart, alone, in terrible isolation. Surely in every sob
Of that despairing moment was my choice made.
Soon, within the hour now, Alcwyn,
The only child, must leave this kitchen's warmth,
Must return, alone, to vast unending death, shrieked
Over jammed muds of an engulphing continent's
Dishonour, and its idiocy, and in two days be dead.
"O God, Christ, why must the darling boy
Now never know that kitchen's tenderness again;
Why must with Alcwyn die dear mother's reason
And dear father's faith, and how, where, why,
Did the power and the glory, tears,
Savagery, and innocence, madness,
Death, and all our agony begin?" I watched
My mother in a thousand kitchens kneel,
Recall those tears wept for me in bedrooms and,
Defenceless, unprepared, hearing that name,
Remember her, and Alcwyn, prayed for and dead, dead,
Dead with sons besought in anguished millions —
At that thirty year unspoken name the mind
Aflame flees screaming from forgotten agony,
From one word's desolation and despair,
While its ignorant indifferent
Utterer walks unmoved away.

Report, Aber, '84

The wintry gull hangs motionless, white above
   The eaten iron of the promenade,
His snowy slicers long and still, the wind's whistle
   Solid as a grit road under his boots.
"All this I read shows", stammers ginger Jasper,
   "A bad poet is a bad poet is not one who writes
Who writes bad poems". "No?" "No. No. All poets do".
   "Oh, shut up, Jasper. You sound like some
Adenoidal Coleridge — 'Sum-m-mject, om-m-mject'."
   "A bad poet never never writes good ones".
"You are a diminisher of that sun, Jasper. It's you
   Who have turned its pale light bleak, sickish,
Its shape smoky. You are a tarnisher of the sea's vast steel".
   "And those Dylan-dead and Aberfan poets, most" he
           munches on,
(Something, somebody, give me great strength!)
   "Most, prove that poetry can not can not arise
From emotion recollected in tranquility".
   The taut elastic of the bay's horizon sags.
"Shut up, Jasper. Shut up. Just leave it out".
   Suspended, the snowy elegance floats up, rises
High in the wind's clear fluids, dawdles, and falls.
   "Only, some times some times from good poets' emotion
Recollected in tranquility". "Jasper, look, listen.
   The wind there shoves the roofed waves over green
Into that vast boiling cuddle below our promenade,
   Each thud booming like a gun gone off in a high pass,
While further out, look, beyond the crash of breakers,
   Smokes rise high and luminous, towering columns
Tall and glittering from the cloisters of the curled sea,
   The bright white spray that, shining, walks inland".
"Great Dafydd's audiences were rings were rings of
           giggling girls".

I flee, wheeling, behind the bored bird, who bends his
        wing,
Curves his snow-white sleeve over the wind's bundle
And bears it skidding sideways up the promenade.

Suicide Note

Flesh:

    All is now forgotten: that unconsuming golden
Glare, the burning beds of sunlit marigolds,
The vision of the fierce high gulls crying,
Poignant and lonely, above our garden,
The panic rictus of the savage milk-white
Greyhounds galloping in thunderous rings
The green grass; silver in bright sunshine's
Equanimity, between the creamy laciness
Of open windows, the vases gleamed,
And great bunches of golden tulips.
How radiant was the lawn, seen
As though sanctified beneath deep
Sunlit snow, how wholesome the smell
                Of sacred bread baking

Unflesh:

    Only the lonely inn-window of the grave
Glowed through my darkness. Between it and the boy
That agony of failure, manhood's wilderness
Where all things created swarm — constantly
They arrive, stand fleetingly before us,
Salute us with their brief signals, beauty,
Horror, meaninglessness, and death,
And endlessly again are changed, become
Things other, in creation's only constancy,
To discontent, effacement, change. I watch
The milk-white antelope outrun, and slain,
Mankind's humiliation, deep wounds, loved
Fingers, hands adored and snatched away, sweetness,
Charm, turned to fury, and in that blackness
Lost, where no great wings beat in redemptive
Flight above me, I disturbed courtyards,

Causeways, nowhere could my hands grope
That half-opened door in at which
I wept to thrust my wounds: and weeping watched
The golden elegance of the young gazelle
Out from the dark green wood approaching —
Fearful, dazzled, on delicate feet, he steps
Into sunshine; the beautiful lioness
In silence rushes through depths of golden
Grass, she leaps, she lands heavily upon him,
Her great weight snaps the bone, the spine breaks
Beneath her with a deadly crack. As he lies
Beside her bleeding, dying, she chews off
His slender haunches — for her cubs his flesh,
The beauty of his face, of the large lustrous eyes,
The delicate nostrils. Pursued, haunted,
I fled further into deserts, which,
In my ignorance, my agony, my failure,
I made for love, for others, yet more bitter,
                    Darker and more desolate.

The Meaning of Fuchsias

The lush valley, the two golden mares
                  loving in the apple orchard,
     The golden-maned for Gwilym, the milky one
          for me,
And through those dark boughs the vast white
               mansion-walls of heaven.
    Why did we not hear, in that treachery
         of sun-varnished windows,
Of handsome clouds, of the fragrant flesh of pears,
              of gull-white moons in their eternal blue,
    And pastures cast out of morning fire
       everywhere brilliant as enamels,
The creeping by of our days, of time,
        of change —
    Only the thrush's hammering of morning
       in the dapples of that sunlight,
And the cupboards of the trees around us
         creaking, creaking.

On the slope the still bushes stood in the sun,
            staring down in silence at their shadows.
    "Fuchsias", said Gwilym, "wild fuchsias" —
      each bush of flowers
The dark glow in my mind still of lit lanterns
         burning crimson through transparencies
               of wine,
    A new delight then, inextinguishable,
      a heart's enduring wonder.

In these sleek gardens, where only meaning
         has no root or blossoming,
    What is it within me stares through its bars
     at fuchsias,

So that I bear again the sudden burden
               of my many dead,
   And you, and all our darkened suns,
             possess me through the doorways of my tears,
You, sanctified listener, who rode by night
               your golden pony
    Through the graveyard, listening,
            and hearing nothing.

Remembering Siani

She leaps in sunlight, her grin wicked —
With all the élan of a French forward
She brings down her blue ball,
Her silky butterscotch coat shedding
A shaken-off golden sheen, a nimbus
Of yellow marigold.
          As children,
In our sunlit kitchen, we gazed down,
Enchanted, into the wonder of the newly opened
Tin of golden syrup — so are her eyes,
Golden, not treacly, darker, more amber,
Warm, firm and clear.
          The barmy Welshman who sold her,
A little thing, to us — how could he? —
Was red-haired, short-legged, bandy and long-nosed,
And so, full-grown, was she; grotesque, absurd,
But yet, beyond belief, and utterly, beautiful.
Dignified too, with a grave clown's dignity,   ·
A comic gravity and grace
That made us want to laugh at her
And yet remain respectful, loving and enthralled.
          Never was she morose, never beat, never
Intimidated by the future, although if I
Was slow to fondle her she could pretend to pout.
          We had once handsome Pompey, a dalmation dog,
A noble creature with a dignity of stance
And grace of movement no short-arsed corgi
Ever could approach — faithful also,
And aloof and stern, but he was often sad,
(Although he died before Hiroshima),
Melancholy, poor boy, and gloomy, deeply
Cast down before the vanity of our human wishes.
          But the little corgi bitch,
Her great uncalculating charm was perpetual,

Full-time, almost professional as a geisha girl's,
But far more innocent and exuberant,
More like a dashing Russian dancer's gaiety,
Leaping uninhibited in jet-black hat of astrakhan
And dishy long green coat and buckskin cossack boots.
But she was Welsh all right, Welsh of the Welsh,
Inbred Welsh, Welsh was her first language
Although she learnt some English too,
Words like *walks*, and *lead*, and *bones* —
And when she ran in rain her coat would smell,
Not of dog, but with the pungency of Teify flannel.
　　Her ancient lineage, from the era of Hywel Dda,
Predated the Welsh Herberts' and Cecils', who, like her kin,
Shot up the social ladder, becoming courtiers
High in royal trust and favour, faithful darlings
Of Elizabeths; some cousins still remain unpaid
And poor auxiliaries of Dyfed cowboys, some are seen
About that tweedy world that tramps with shooting sticks
Across the pages of the posher magazines;
Some are yet short peasants predominant in palaces.
　　When our memories,
Much that we recall, more we are haunted by,
Is shameful, is of loss and tears, suffering and death —
Blessings upon the miracle of Siani, comical, even absurd,
But handsome always, faithful, loving, droll,
Who by living, being, gave poor us delight,
Who, in a morning's sunlight, would run white-bibbed
Towards us, across the glittering lawn, grinning,
Her snow-white paws scattering sunlit
Dewdrops, scattering diamonds.

Prologue and Three Fragments

Seven keys to Shaderdom

(Let us call him) Tom, Tom ap Twm, Shader Tom, Tom Didymus, tree and landscape specialist, painter, ex-and failed, enters his attic lodgings through the striped wooden door, painted in broad bendy zebra bands of black and white and, supported by his ashen thumb-stick, limps his evening circuit of his room, which is lofty, large, spacious even, but comfortless, draughty, bare and chaotically littered, i.e. bachelor. Studio-cum-living-room-cum-kitchen-cum-bed-room.

Echoes in the attic abound, they reverbrate loudly every-where from floor-boards to roofslates, the hollow has the resonance of a gigantic skull.

On one of the long sides, the slates of almost half the cobwebby roof have been removed and replaced between the rafters, thus forming one enormous window, by panes of north-facing glass. But the clarity of this glass has been much reduced by a coating of atmospheric filth and, since the roof appears to stand directly beneath the pathway of the south-bound migrants, by a thick plastering of bird droppings. This vast window Shader calls his sky-light and over it during darkness he is able, to preserve his privacy, to draw a khaki curtain draped on a brass rod with wooden rings, at, like the roof, an angle of forty-five degrees.

Beneath the skylight still stand a kitchen armchair, an easel, his useless throne of orange boxes.

A small naked electric light bulb, 25w., hangs down on a thread-like wire, furry with dust, from one of the rafters.

Several rows of leaning canvases, paintings of various sizes and shapes, all thick with dust and unframed, are turned to face the attic walls, which are stone built and knee high and appear to have once received a watery coat of whitewash; these winding queues of pictures stretch back across the attic floor, they stand patiently as though waiting at secret exits that, opened, will allow them to flock out and take wing into the external world.

Right across the whitelimed gable wall stretches a wide band of graffiti in a colourful chaos — many words and drawings superimposed one upon the other in the manner of primitive cave-paintings; sketches of trees, branches, leaves, fruit, in charcoal, crayon, pencil; short poems hung on a vast Tree of Knowledge; memos; obiter dicta; pencilled caricatures of great spirit haloed with telephone numbers or with addresses ballooning from their mouths. In red chalk snatches such as,

> *My name is Twm Pryce,*
> *My feet are like ice*
> *In this bloody attic,*
> *And that's emphatic.*

"A painter is in a bad way if his mind works only when he is working it": "The heart has tears which the mind rejects"; "Poor Chestie; married, he has become a sponge-spine"; "Open the window", cried the dying king, "honour and compassion must suffice"; "Oh, milky antelope, oh, perfumed nard"; "Who will instruct me now in the faculty of my defence?"; "The vulnerable brow emerges into battle"; "I hate shy people — frustrated show-offs".

Ignoring these revelations Shader watches once more, enthralled and incredulous, the wooden, easel-like rigidity of his own advance over the gritty floorboards — leaning heavily on his snake-tongued thumbstick — upon his frequently collided with, knocked flat and well-cracked cheval mirror. His approach, observed with his solitary eye, the sight of which, despite gross over-use, remains unimpaired, appals and distresses him. He is grotesque. Apart from his grey helmet-like headgear he is dressed in a style, not bohemian, not artistic, but vaguely hippodamous, appropriate to one proposing to attend some remote rural horseshow and to gain admission without paying — thick-soled brown boots, or rather boot, short khaki gaiters over black corduroy trousers, lovat-green calf-length tweed overcoat heavily fouled and clouted and slackly belted with orangebox rope, and a brightly coloured yellow neckerchief. One of his feet is bedroom slippered, the toes bare.

He limps among the chaos covering the knotted floorboards (which are the attic's only shelves) — many books in toppled columns; a pile of still rolled-up and unopened newspapers ditto; on a short trestle table several cardboard grocery boxes containing unused tubes of paint; sheaves of brushes in jamjars and a wooden palette, home-made from the side of a butterbox, stand in the bosh; two or three stacks of unused canvases lean beside the throne; on the floor are dropped widely strewn used rags, paint-stained; flattened paint tubes and collections of empty medium bottles and flagons litter the skylight's long cill; in one corner is heaped a pile of old clothes, grey under thick dust; outside the scarlet-painted wardrobe, used as a pantry, its door panels gilded, stand a stack of saucepans, a kettle, a teapot, a fryingpan, a porringer and a precarious pyramid of soup tins; a black jacket hangs over the back of a deckchair.

The pervasive smell of the attic is of fried bacon regularly burnt.

Before going out Shader has lit the gas stove oven, the door of which now stands wide open for warmth.

He has painted in oils on the floorboards beside his bed a brilliant oblong representation of a Persian rug of vivid colouring and intricate and symbolic design, the tangled cream fringes of which, especially, are rendered with delusive realism. Untying his rope girdle and discarding on to the bed his tweed overcoat, he puts on from the deckchair his black velvet jacket with the buttons of yellow china. He drops his *thumbstick noisily upon his painted carpet and sinks down, sighing loudly with relief, on his back, along his red carthen-covered daybed. Having hoisted up his lame leg with both hands into a position of comfort and repose upon it he again sinks back in sight of his mirror. Reclining thus, he resumes his daily questionings, his contemplation of his face and form, he considers once more his surroundings, his cyclothymia and the vicissitudes of his long and hapless life.*

In the interest of increased comfort he removes his hat from his head to his chest.

★ ★ ★

Shader, unable to sleep, and browsing through his heap of books, has a vision of fair women, his own country's and others', which recalls the sighs of his, as he believes, wasted youth.

Where is Tangwen now, where Nest, where is Gwenllian,
The apple-blossom and the summer's glow?
Where are the "gentle, gold-torqued maidens
Of this Island"? Where is Elen of the Hosts?
Sun-bright Elen under her diadem,
Gold and rubies and imperial stones?
Mantled Elen in her milk-white silk, clasped
And girdled with red gold — yellow-haired Elen
Of excelling beauty, on her golden throne,
Her cheek upon her sleeping Emperor's cheek?
Where is Lleucu now, where Gwen, where golden
Angharad?
Where are Betty Blythe, and Vilma Banki, and Laura La
Plante?
Where Eryl, the goddess — her stare,
Her hauteur, that we, her worshippers, believed could halt

Chemistry at the confines of her body?
Where Rhiannon, enchantress, whose beauty crashed
about our flesh,
Blazing, golden as shattered nets of torn-down
Lightnings to catch us thunderstruck and staggered?
Slake me in moon-showers, cool Llio, crazy, I cried,
Wipe me in rainbows of your moon-mist loveliness.
Where is Olwen, where Branwen, where Brengain?
Where Morfydd — her honeyed hair, her unshawled
shoulders,
Her marbled arms, beneath which nature,
With accustomed insensitivity,
Had placed a heavy tuft of low-grade hair?
Where is Pola Negri — Pola, the tingle of your teeth
Like calvary, your lips like couches?
Where all the beautiful and high-class girls
Who let us finger them in the dark lanes of our village?
I have seen them since, tired in city supermarkets,
Thick-nosed, afflicted, grey, called Nana, buying
Cut-price toilet rolls in large quantities.
And lovely Mabli of the mental hospitals,
Mabli, dying alone in smelling sun, in the glass
Corridors of her mind's reclusion,
Grey-bearded, her lids down, silently
Wetting herself — and my voice brings back some
Tapping past upon her heart's abandoned panes,
And the anguished inmate, wild-eyed exile,
Rouses, croaking, "Jesus Christ, the same
Yesterday, today, and for ever", — where
Is her lovely striding, her high laugh, her molten
Leopard-leap of wit and silken winds lifting
Her gold-red hair, sea-winds above her ears
Lifting that sunlight polished gold, word-
Drowning breeze between us on the sunlit beach —

And I awake again to hear, "Jesus Christ, the same
Yesterday, today, and for ever", — and
I feel the shit-soaked feathers beat about my head,
The screeches wake me and the talons tear my heart.

*As Shader rises, weeping, to close and replace his
Mabinogion, his glance alights upon a cywydd couplet in a
book of poems fallen open from the untidy pile heaped beside
his bed on the attic floor.*

Pa beth ydyw byw a bod?
Nwyd ofer, yna difod.

* * *

*Shader, having returned to his attic after a session of
watching Soaptruck's television during a visit to the floor
below, lies on his bed confused and outraged at what he has
seen. This has been his first viewing of the new medium and the
effect of its beautiful vividness and almost palpable horror
upon him has been to set his spirit into a state of agonised
turmoil. Never again will he subject himself to such an hour of
confused torment.*

Beautiful the beeches' anger in autumn's burn.
Beautiful the loose mouth of the torn corn-poppy's
scarlet,
The delicate dawn embrace of glittering night-spun
webwork,
The landing glide on cooling lakes of sea-duck.
Out of the golden block of uncut wheat thundered
Loud in sunlight blood of the trapped hare,
And the blood-soaked shadows rose, as the dead, the
children,

Swarmed screaming across the shattered sunlight of every
        broken wall.

Beautiful the fragile roof of ice, frail frost-white
      Glass of winter, lacing the cart-tracks; sea-tons
      Thunderous against quaking embankments,
Storm-sea in the high air tearing its lace,
And the sharp wince of the overwhelmed sea-crag,
          drowned
      Beneath the elaborate arm of the breaker.
      Vast heaven was small everywhere, and happened
        less, and drowned
Blood was not remitted, not in whatever tears or prayers.

Beautiful the papery crocuses, pure white, purple, or
        luminous rust,
      Buds of amber, golden beads, the burnished
      Cups and long gold globes unbroken — crocuses
Encrusting green grass like golden cakes of perfume.
Spring, and over the lawns, soon, the first cold hoarfrost of
        daisies,
      Heaped hedgerows overwhelmed in maybloom —
        beautiful
      Their cream-crested billows, or, crimson, dark
        breakers of corroding blood
While our child dies bleeding, alone, on the sun-splashed,
        the well-bombed road.

Summer again and the flat incoming tides endlessly
      Floating their milky meadows on to the beaches;
      Parkland oaks were filled with breeze, were effortlessly
Lifted up in the slow-motion of taking-off waterbirds;
Beautiful the slide of cloud shadows, dark sheets
      Of prowling smokes pushed flat across sun-bright

pastures
While our sanctuaries smoked, were defiled, were acrid
And ablaze, the mind's appalled ruins swarmed
With the screams of all the silent, the dead, the shadowless,
The paunched skeletons, the gourd-skulls, the
fly-sucked eyes,
And when in the guise of mother, I, childless, heard
The screeches of my burning child, meaninglessness itself
was then
Without all meaning, was become vain, barren, dead and
meaningless.

A hail shower falls on Shader's window panes and slowly slides down the glass thick as a gruel, blotting out blooms and branches.

★   ★   ★

Shader recalls being abandoned, asleep, by his art college friends, in the bar of the dockland pub, the King's Arms, with its three blonde barmaids in their tight white knitted jumpers. He ultimately finds himself, in the small hours, alone in a deserted city square where an icy brightness fell, a bleak disk of illumination, on the pavement round the base of a concrete lamp-post. Sea-winds swilled the dockland cobbles, lifting dust, and above the slum- square squalor a lurching plane tree sprawled up black, blown abroad, bare, tangly, stiff like dirty hair.

Thus it was in indolence, in darkness, drunk,
I watched intently nothing, and in the anguish
Of a passing calm, that pause, that place, the stridencies,
Inveterate visitants, resumed; visions, remembrances,
Splendours, wounds — those unending rituals

Of bloom, leaf, berry and death,
Solstice, equinox and death,
    Systole, diastole and death.

            A long lit block, the last black tram,
            Pier-head bound, swept
            Clanging into the square
            And, beside the cold lamp's
            Light-cone, halted clamour
            With its hiss.

I thought, — Sober, I cannot now dissever even
        Past victories from those past confederates, past
                    defeats —
All that vast blur, harsh and unalterable imprint, spreads
        Through a universe, and limitless unpeopled epochs,
Bleak immutability, beyond the hope of prayer.

Oh, sudden splashed sea-milk, watched, recalled in ecstasy,
        Crashed lavish under sunlight across a child's red rocks;
Spring's sunlit slopes of boyhood, perfumed,
        Deep blue with bluebells like a tilted lake;
A chandelier of heaven's radiance, massed, once,
        Upon one golden pasture in the brown
Velvet of a sombre hill — once, sweet to my staring
        As an ebbing agony, gold, poured gold, upon the dusty
                    plushes
Of a Valleys slope; the mirrored swans slow-skating,
        Sliding a silken white and silences across
The pond's black glass, or polished river, or mercury lake —
        . . . *holl hyfrydwch natur,*
        A'i melystra penna'i maes,
        All meaningless now — not meaningless, still

Yielding their insistent sweetnesses, but ineffectual,
　　No solace in such blissfulness for the past's guilt,
Its degradation, shames, the future's horrors — in such
　　Dazzling remembered brevities no liberation,
No intimations and no hope.

　　　Suddenly a seaman and his woman, sullen,
　　　Common, heavy, middle-aged, dull,
　　　Moved hob-nailed out and luminous from near
　　　Shadows. He boarded the panting tram, she
　　　Lifted up for him his heavy seaman's kit-bag.

Young, I, a spurner of correction, one who had declined
　　To bear that killing burden of another's dreams,
Packed out with feverish scruples my reluctances, with
　　　great Art,
　　　Cared nothing then for happiness but ecstasy, not
　　　sadness
Only terror and despair before the universal diligence
　　Of flesh, its zest, its vast futility.
The unbelievable and millionth fieldmouse foetus, doomed,
　　　Growing in secrecy its pearly fingernails — pipefish
　　　and mudfish,
All death-bound, monsters, creatures of malignancy and
　　　horror;
　　　That torment of engulphing space, eternal glitter of
　　　ice boulders
Circling, endlessly bright, implacable, some planet's
　　　brilliancy —
　　　All, all, creatures and creations, pursuing blind,
　　　unfaltering,
Obdurate, the indifference of their unimaginable
　　　purposes —
　　　All this eternally, while you, dear brother, here,

Saintly and uxorious, unmerited embracer, gentler, of
       faithless bones,
    After your God's grace sermon you walk in darkness
        your road home
Alone, manse-ward, weeping, to that wayward cancerous
       wife.
    Could you, could any, hear that admonition, gentle,
        loving,
Through time's ferocities, vacuity of distances, seethe of
       stars,
    To the stunned heart intoned, "My child, my child,
        peace, don't cry, don't cry"?
Where, brother, where was your comforting? All my
       compassion could,
    But did not, proffer then — the hard-won terrors of a
        manhood's disbelief.

      The wife heaved aboard the heavy kit-bag.
      Woman and sailor nodded, smiled, kissed briefly,
        solemnly,
      The tram slid on, increasing a muffled clanging
      Through the night's black felt. She,
      Standing in the lamplight, waving, then turned,
      Walked sobbing back, and sobbing passed me, now
      In my shadows, sober, invisible, alone
      With bladderwrack tree, and clockwork rats,
        and dockland filth.

Eyes shed their tears. That is all, the alpha and omega,
    That despairing radiance is our scant certainty, all we
        know.
A squalid sea-dawn spread dimly ochre, an apricot glue,
    Behind the street lamp's bush of rain.

I shuffled, shouldering my bogus intellectual hump,
    Home to my painting,
And the aching pages of my poetry, and prayer.

*Outside the skylight the sun rises red, smouldering in
swirls of static black clouds, and smoking like a burnt
hayrick.*

* * * * * *

The above three fragments are parts of a long poem consisting, when
completed, of seven sections.

Envoi

Old, I watched the darling swallow families gathering,
Their fringes perched, spaced out, along high village wires,
Each sweet bird black, no wider than an eyelash — why
Should these bring molten to my throat so old a heart?

Blessing, I saw their swift flight above radiant hayfields,
    it was warm
And summer then, in hundreds they wove their invisible
    silkiness above
The standing hay (their weft swift, it was the *wennol* of
    the waterside weavers),
Or they ruggered unstoppable down wings of the blinding
    meadows,
They were reckless, their headlong speed, as though
    defying calamity, rocked them — "Be careful,
Dear things", I wished to cry out in warning at such
    consummate lunacy —
The wheezing machinery of their tiny cries the sweetest
    of birdsong;
Black and white in their beauty, in their rashness they
    licked out sleek wings,
They were dark, they were glossy, rigid the symmetry of
    their forked tail feathers.

Now it is all over. They gather on the high wires
    twittering in excitement
To be gone in this gloom. Goodbye, you were the lovely,
    white lilac birds,
Your flocks flying in to our wastelands trawled here
    warmth
From the longed-for south, from the lands where sunlight
    falls
Bright on dark skins, brilliant on the beauty of the dappled
    antelope,

On olives and honey, balm, oil and barley — early figs
Are there also and heavy gold leaking everywhere from
        sunlit trees.
Goodbye, goodbye, you were about us in sunlight, swift,
Bright as the astonishment of youthful perceptions —
        lovely as glancing epiphanies
The gaiety of your visitations; and now you prepare joy-
        fully to leave us,
Heedless you take off for ever, you are visions and images,
The words and their dazzle, you leave me bereft, darling
        birds,
You will plunge elate under rainbows, forgetful of us beneath
        great girders of the grey clouds —
Where did you ponder the gospels of that strict navigation? —
Night travellers joyful among jewelled harness of darkness,
Hurling yourselves at hot suns risen smoking before you,
Or burying brilliance in the panes of their waters, and you
Exultant between emptiness blue above and blue below you.

Mist and darkness begin now to gather and the small rain
        falls heavily —
And here with the sad, with the finished, fleeting enchanters,
        you leave me,
With the rain, and the ruffian wind rising, and these shabby
        old men standing bowed all about me —
Who are these grey mutterers? — ach, hateful, rancid,
With thick glasses and ear-plugs, white hairs and holes in
        their trousers —
Oh, birds, darling thieves and bewitchers, at your going
        we are weary, sad,
We are sick and defeated, all are abandoned, with tears
        on our cheeks
And with great weights heavy on our hearts.